HURRICANE HARVEY

HOUSTON AND HEROISM

Celebrating the Compassion,
Caring and *Goodness*
of Ethical Intelligence in Action

JOHN T. OPINCAR

Cultural Fire Press, LLC
Houston, Texas
www.harveybook.org

Houston, Texas

Copyright © 2018 by John T. Opincar

All rights reserved. In accordance with the U. S. Copyright Act of 1976, the scanning, uploading and electronic sharing of any part of this book without permission of the publisher constitute unlawful piracy and theft of the author's intellectual property. If you would like to use material from the book (other than for review purposes), prior written permission must be obtained by contacting the publisher at permissions@culturalfirepress.com.

Thank you for your support of the author's rights.

Cultural Fire Press, LLC
Houston, Texas
www.culturalfirepress.com

Printed in the United States of America

First Edition: August, 2018

10 9 8 7 6 5 4 3 2 1

You may contact the author at john.opincar@boardroompartners.com.

Cover and interior design by Brett Miller, www.bjm-bookdesign.com.

Cover background photo by Pulitzer Prize-winning photojournalist Marcus Yam

The publisher is not responsible for websites (or their content) that are not owned by the publisher.

Library of Congress Cataloging-in-Publication Data has been applied for.

ISBN: 978-0-9980890-2-7

Photo Courtesy of KTRK TV

This book is dedicated to and celebrates the ethically intelligent life of Sergeant Steve Perez, a 34-year Houston Police Department veteran, who gave his life in serving others during hurricane Harvey in Houston. Police Chief Art Acevedo called Sergeant Perez "a sweet and gentle public servant."

CELEBRATING THE COMPASSION, CARING, AND

CONTENTS

Contents — v
Foreword — ix
Acknowledgments — xiii

Introduction — 1
    This is Houston — 7
    The Home Invader Who Refused to Leave — 11
    Harvey Water aka "the Water" — 12
    Harvey Brain aka "The Moment" — 15

Chapter 1: Breathing Goodness — 19
    My Prayer Warrior — 23
    A Soul-Etching Visit — 28
    Houston's Gift — 41

Chapter 2: Seeing Others Clearly — 47
    Do You See Me? — 49
    Worldview Windows — 52
    Diversity is Not Division — 60

Chapter 3: Living In Truth — 63
    Moments of Truth — 66
    What is Truth? — 72
    Truth and Consequences — 76

Chapter 4: Serving In Silence — 79
    Gratitude, Currency of the Universe — 82
    Unsung Heroes, Unexpected Relationships — 87
    Gratitude Opens and Sustains Relationships. — 93

Chapter 5: Finding Peace In Purpose — 99
- Water, Water Everywhere — 100
- Calm Before, During and After — 112
- Purity Of Purpose Rarely Seen — 116

Chapter 6: Knowing and Doing Right — 123
- Finding True North — 126
- Ethical Comfort Zone — 132
- Walking Away — 137

Chapter 7: It's Okay to Cry — 141
- Embracing an Ancient Partner — 144
- Drenched in Water and Emotions — 148
- Engine of Life — 156

Chapter 8: Leading From The Eye Of The Storm — 163
- The First Two Casualties Are . . . — 165
- Play-By-Play of an Unfolding Disaster — 173
- And—The Winners Are… — 190

Chapter 9: Sweating Underwater — 191
- Fighting The Futility — 192
- Testing Our Trust — 199
- Sweating the Strategy — 204

Chapter 10: Celebrating Goodness — 209
- Seeing the Spirit — 212
- Victors Not Victims — 216
- Lifting the Good — 222

Chapter 11: Crumbling Silos — 233
- Mending the Hurt — 234
- A Harbinger — 240

CONTENTS

Birthing a Goodness Revolution ... 241
Conclusions and Recommendations ... 247

Harvey Heroes aka "The Unsung" ... 250

The Journey From Truth To Wisdom Graphic ... 260

Discussion Questions For Us ... 261

Photo Credits ... 263

About the Author ... 267

Other Books By The Author ... 269

CELEBRATING THE COMPASSION, CARING, AND

FOREWORD

Last August and September the world got a glimpse of the mettle of Houston's people as the relentless rain of hurricane Harvey brought historic flooding, anxious suffering, abundant altruism, premature deaths and love and compassion.

It is the love and compassion that Dr. John Opincar focuses on in this book. He calls it ethical intelligence, an essential component of the human experience that drives us to a common good and a place of shared caring for one another. While he watched police officers sacrifice their lives, neighbors grab boats to help strangers, donations grow mountain high, shelters spring to life and grand displays of kind-heartedness on a scale of millions of people, Dr. Opincar made an instant decision,

He leaned over to his wife and announced his intentions— "I'm watching what I've been researching for ten years, and that's human ethical intelligence, people being good to one another. I've got to write a book about this as a celebration of what we did!" —he told me when I interviewed him after the storm. In this book, Dr. Opincar shares his insights about the call of our better angels. He was inspired in this quest by the amazing courage and goodness of Houston's people.

During this time of heroes, mine was named Richard Gerlovich. I spent Harvey's visit on the radio as a news anchor at KTRH, Houston's massive and legendary 50,000-watt AM news giant that has covered Texas hurricanes and storms for more than 85 years. I wasn't in the original broadcast plan. But, there I was, leaping into live-around-the-clock-anchored storm coverage on the Friday morning before the storm made landfall because our Corpus Christi affiliate was evacuating and needed to simulcast our signal.

We broadcasters are an odd lot—when danger threatens we run toward microphones attached to transmitters to save lives. It's what we do. My partner, Scott Crowder, and I jumped into action and started getting things lined up. We couldn't have been more prepared that Friday in late August. We had been training for years and were armed with a white, loose-leaf binder labeled, *KTRH Hurricane Manual,* that weighed in at more than five pounds and included every detail of hurricane science. Everything was exactly in place—except me. Allow me to explain.

Our morning anchor of six years, Shara Fryer's partner and our center of gravity, Matt Patrick died July 9th. For 15 months, Matt courageously fought a savage, voracious metastatic cancer while broadcasting on-air. Matt did his last show on a Thursday and died that Sunday. We were unrecovered, still grieving and mourning from that painful loss when hurricane Harvey hit. As a result, the radio station was short-handed. It fell to me, a weekend news anchor, to step up and assist Scott during daylight hours.

A 40-year well-traveled gypsy radio veteran, I'd been in San Francisco when the 7.1 magnitude World Series earthquake hit in '89, killing 66 people. I was on the air for 12 hours in Nashville as thirteen tornadoes destroyed the downtown area, killing seven. I anchored during 9/11. I thought I was ready.

Live coverage of disasters is in my bailiwick and I knew enough to fill my email inbox with facts and information—a map of the Gulf coast cone where Hurricane Harvey was expected to hit, a map of Corpus Christi, weather alerts, contact names and numbers, press releases, hurricane vernacular and evacuation plans and routes.

When staring down a Category 4 hurricane and lives are on the line, no information is too insignificant. So, I sent myself everything possible. Then after entering the control room brimming with confidence—it all fell apart.

With one eye I watched the clock tick down. But, with the other eye I couldn't find the email icon on the computer before me. I was using Matt Patrick's computer, and it didn't access my email. I was completely unarmed, empty-handed, aghast and panicked. The blood in my brain drained as the red on-air light came on. My mouth was moving and words were coming out. I felt like I was drowning when I felt the arms of our Director of IT Richard Gerlovich reach over me and begin tapping on the keyboard. In a few moments, my email popped up, and **I was saved, rescued!**

I hope to never forget the feeling of being awash with gratitude and uplifted by another's impromptu kindness. That sensation of being rescued or rescuing others became the coin of Harvey's realm and the common denominator of we Houston Harvey survivors. During the eleven days of storm coverage, as I called for more boats, directed neighbors to shelters and commuters to open roads, took phone calls from people on rooftops daring death as waters rose, interviewed governors and mayors, judges, senators and congressmen and the Flood District's Jeff Lindner repeatedly, not one of those days went by that I didn't stop to think of Richard Gerlovich.

As the Cajun Navy joined Houstonians pulling 17,000 people from floodwaters, as Addicks and Barker reservoirs spilled over their banks adding to the 100,000+ submerged homes and as more than 80 souls left this earth, I identified most with those being rescued.

What prompts us to goodness? Why do we rescue others? Why are people good? This book is an examination of what those in a position to assist others did and insight into why they did it.

Dr. Opincar's own son-in-law, Sammy, was among them, one of those nameless volunteers who became an unsung hurricane Harvey hero. Sammy asked a group of strangers if there was a way to help. "They put Sammy on a rescue boat with a guy and his dog, and three retired United States Marines, including a woman warrior, and went out and rescued people for four days." Dr. Opincar told me, proudly.

Hurricane Harvey lingers in our memories as a collection of rescues and heroes, now brought together in a book that reminds us of who we were when it counted and inspires us to remain true to the potential of who we can be.

Nikki Courtney
Reporter and News Anchor
KTRH NewsRadio
Houston, Texas
June, 2018

ACKNOWLEDGMENTS

Although this book bears my name as author, it would have never become a reality without the help of many others. Following is a partial list of those to whom I am forever indebted for this book's creation.

- *My Lord and Savior Jesus Christ whose continued inspiration and spiritual sustenance made this book possible.*
- *My soulmate Linda, who is an ever-present helpful advisor, critic, encourager, supporter, proofreader, life partner, peacemaker and prayer-warrior!*
- *My Lakewood Church family, especially Pastor John Gray, whose outward public emotional reaction to the tragedy of hurricane Harvey reinforced my own.*
- *My friend and colleague, Dr. David Breslauer, whose work in the "trenches" makes him an unsung hero of this work.*
- *Debra Engle, my literary counsel, editor, and copyrighter, who is always available for providing just the "write" answer. www.debraengle.com.*
- *Brett Miller, artist and designer, who donated the cover for this work.*
- *The community and business leaders who not only led this community with distinction during hurricane Harvey and its aftermath but also graciously shared their time and perspectives with me as I wrote this book. I gratefully present the following names in alphabetical order.*
- *Chief Art Acevedo, Chief of Police, City of Houston*
- *Mr. Alan Bernstein, Director of Communications, City of Houston Mayor's Office*

- Ms. Nikki Courtney, KTRH NewsRadio Anchor and Reporter
- Mr. Scott Crowder, KTRH NewsRadio Anchor and Reporter
- Judge Robert Eckels, Former Harris County Judge
- Judge Ed Emmett, Director of Homeland Security and Emergency Management and Harris County Judge
- Mr. Bryan Erickson, Director of AM Programming for iHeartMedia in Houston
- Mr. W. Carl Glaw, CPA, Founder & Managing Partner, GLO CPAs, LLLP
- Ms. Linda R. Glaw, Firm Administrator, GLO CPAs, LLLP
- Ms. Dawn Gillespie, Governance and Business Manager, Houston Grand Opera
- Sheriff Ed Gonzalez, Harris County Sheriff
- Mr. Bob Harvey, President and CEO, Greater Houston Partnership
- Mr. Perryn Leech, Managing Director, Houston Grand Opera
- Mr. Jeff Lindner, Chief Meteorologist, Harris County Flood Control District
- Chief Richard Mann, Executive Assistant Fire Chief, City of Houston
- Chief Samuel Peña, Fire Chief, City of Houston
- Mr. Willie Rios, Mayor pro tem, City of South Houston
- Mr. Jason Ryan, Director, U.S. Media Affairs, BP America
- Mr. Francisco Sánchez, Jr., Deputy Emergency Management Coordinator for Harris County Office of Homeland Security & Emergency Management
- Ms. Lisa Shumate, Associate Vice President and General Manager, Houston Public Media
- Honorable Sylvester Turner, Mayor, City of Houston
- Dr. Cesare Wright, President Kino-Eye Center, Leadership and Outreach Specialist and Lecturer Rice University Center for Engineering Leadership

- Ms. Cindy Yeilding, Senior Vice President, BP America

Although we refer to them as "Admin", "Executive Assistant" or "Secretary," these are the people who keep our world running. This book would not be what it is without their assistance. They are, in alphabetic order by last name:

- Ms. Leanna Abbott, Executive Assistant to Harris County Judge Ed Emmett who is also Director of Homeland Security and Emergency Management
- Ms. Linae Acquisto, Assistant to Greater Houston Partnership CEO Bob Harvey
- Ms. Victoria Cordova, Communications Manager, Office of Lisa Shumate, Houston Public Media
- Ms. Maria Davis, Administrative Specialist, Scheduling, Office of Mayor Sylvester Turner
- Ms. Denise Estrada, Assistant to Houston Fire Chief Peña Ms. Lydia Gonzales, Assistant to Houston Police Chief Acevedo
- Ms. Stacey Krecmer, Executive Assistant to BP America Senior Vice President Cindy Yeilding
- Ms. Adriana Perez, Assistant to Harris County Sheriff Gonzalez
- Darci Stavinoha, Assistant Firm Administrator, GLO CPAs, LLLP
- Ms. Veronica Weatherspoon, Division Manager, Office of Mayor Sylvester Turner
- Every hurricane Harvey survivor, first responder and civilian rescuer who selflessly shared their experiences with me. Their stories made this work possible.

INTRODUCTION

Rescuers Evacuating People from Flooded Homes

"Momma, Momma, Momma breathe!" Screamed the woman to the motionless figure just lifted into the rocking boat.

"We've been rescued! It's going to be okay now!" No response.

Sandra and her mother had just been rescued by a couple of nameless guys in a flat bottom boat. Sandra was wading in chest-deep water next to the boat. The tropical-force wind was driving the rain sideways.

One of the guys, wearing nothing but swimming trunks and a hat, yelled for Sandra to get into the boat because they had to move on to the next house. She shrieked,

"I can't! The water is too deep!"

The other guy in the boat reached over and grabbed her hands. They both struggled for what seemed an interminable amount of time. Finally, with the boat listing badly and rocking wildly, Sandra clambered onto the boat. Sandra moved over next to her mother and screamed again,

Rooftop Flooding Near Author's Home

"Breathe, breathe! We've been rescued! It's okay. These nice men have saved our lives!" This time, a weak smile emerged from Momma's face.

As the relentless rain continued to sting everyone in the boat, the two nameless guys and their passengers moved on to the next house, and then the next, and then the next. By the end of that day, this one small boat and two nameless guys rescued dozens of people from a flooded Houston neighborhood.

This short story was repeated thousands of times during the five days that hurricane Harvey, then tropical storm Harvey, punished the greater Houston metropolitan area with high winds and more than **47 inches of rain.**

> They just saw their neighbors in peril and responded without regard to their own well-being and any potential reward.

These two nameless guys were not first responders, at least as far as we know. They just saw their neighbors in peril and responded without regard to their own well-being and any potential reward. They used their own boat, fuel, and time and did what they could for people they had never met and, most likely, would never see again. Sandra and her mother breathed goodness that day. It was the beginning of **Houston's defining moment.**

A 42,000-Year Event. Hurricane Harvey made landfall near Rockport, Texas during the night hours of August 25, 2017 as a category four storm packing sustained winds of 130 mph. Although the wind and flood damage within a 100-mile radius of landfall was substantial, Harvey produced unprecedented flooding further up the coast in Southeast Texas, including the greater Houston metropolitan area.

The greater Houston metropolitan area, which is spread out over several counties and dozens of municipalities, is home to over 6.9 million people who drive an estimated 3.3 million cars. Harvey caused a five-day rain event, cited by some experts as a once-every-42,000-year occurrence, that dumped over **four feet of rain** before moving east into Louisiana. The resultant flooding destroying an estimated one million cars and more than 260,000 homes and businesses.

This book is my first-hand account of someone who personally lived it. My family and I have lived in Texas for over 40 years, most of that time in the greater Houston metropolitan area. Although my personal home was surrounded by multiple feet of water, the water never entered my home. The rest of my neighbors weren't so fortunate. Many were rescued by boats, National

Guard vehicles, and Coast Guard helicopters. And, many suffered great personal losses, mostly uninsured.

My family was blessed in that none of our four households suffered any serious damages from the flooding. As a result, many family members became involved in various aspects of helping the community. As I was trapped in my home for two days because of the water, I couldn't offer any direct physical assistance. Beyond that, I am not mentally inclined nor sufficiently physically gifted to work on a rescue boat in waist-deep water, as pictured nearby. Nonetheless, I wanted to make a lasting contribution to the community.

As I surveyed the damage and watched our community's response to it, I was overwhelmed with pride and gratitude. What I also saw was a phenomenon that always makes an appearance during these kinds of tragic human events. It's a special kind of goodness and caring for our fellow humans that is an intrinsic part of our human nature, usually submerged and hidden within our consciousness. But, the breadth and depth of that goodness and caring was generously palpable and, even by Texas standards—**epic**.

Of the many gifts God has given me, researching and writing are two that give me great satisfaction. As I continued breathing the goodness of the events unfolding before me, I realized—I knew what this was! It was something I've researched and written about for more than a decade. It was our **human ethical intelligence** manifesting itself right before my eyes! In our troubled and polarized world, it's rare to see such a prolific and public display of this ancient gift. It was at that moment, that I knew I had to write this book.

So, here's our story, the story of Hurricane Harvey, Houston and Heroism.

While acknowledging the acute hardship and suffering caused by hurricane Harvey's aftermath, this book is not about suffering, hardship, and tragedy. I've included some of that in this book because it deserves acknowledgment. But, someone else will write that account.

This book is a **CELEBRATION** of the triumphant emergence of a long-dormant and ancient human gift that is at least as old as the 4500-year-old pyramid at Giza—our human **Ethical Intelligence!** We see the outward manifestations of this gift whenever a human tragedy unfolds anywhere on the planet. But, Houston's ethically intelligent response to hurricane Harvey was especially instructive and deserves memorialization.

This book is full of stories of heroism, self-sacrifice, altruism, benevolence, love, and human goodness. The people of Houston and others who came from all over the world to help showed what our human *ethical intelligence looks like in action.* Hurricane Harvey and its aftermath in Texas created a vivid movie set

Houston Metropolitan Area Underwater

or a stage from which I have told the hopeful story of our human ethical intelligence, as seen through the lens of this tragedy.

Researching and writing this book was a labor of love. It's my gift to our community. My fondest hope is the profits generated from this book will help the survivors of hurricane Harvey's flooding, many that I've personally met over the months since that tragedy struck our community. The bravery, generosity, love and just plain goodness of the people who live and work in this metropolitan area is something the **world must hear about.** We showed that living together in love and peace is possible!

Although I try to remain hopefully optimistic, I recognize we live in a world with a short attention span. In the grand sweep of history, today's news stories occupy but a few nanoseconds of time. And, so it is the case with our Houston Harvey story. Recognizing this reality and the fact that our story has a short "sell by date," I've researched and written this book as quickly as possible.

I've tried to use public domain photographs whenever possible. I've made a diligent good-faith effort to obtain permission to use those few photographs appearing in this book that are not in the public domain. If I've inadvertently used your photograph without first obtaining permission, please accept my apology. All photography credits appear in the Photo Credits table at the back of the book.

I've included many stories in this book. Most of these stories I've personally heard from survivors, volunteers, first responders, leaders and public officials. I've also included stories from third parties, published and unpublished accounts and others. I've tried to include as many as possible and keep the book a reasonable length. The names and locations in these stories were changed to protect privacy, a promise I made to everyone who shared with me. Stories from public officials and leaders are directly attributed to them.

This book also contains "direct quotes" from material that was taken from transcripts of recorded conversations. As you can imagine, conversations tend to meander a bit. Words get repeated. Thoughts get disconnected. Connecting words like "and" are freely used. Most people would find reading actual direct quotes from such material frustrating and boring. As result, I've "cleansed" directly quoted material for your enjoyment. In those cases, neither the meaning nor the context was altered.

Houston and the surrounding metropolitan area is an amazing place. Here are some facts about our great city you may not know or remember.

This Is Houston

Houston is a city that should've never been created, at least in its current location. Many have said Houston is built on a swamp, or,

Downtown Houston at Dusk 2017

in modern terminology, a floodplain! They were forewarned of their folly, but the Allen brothers, two New York land speculators, did it anyway. Thank God they did! Because Houston is now one of the most vibrant metropolises in the world.

> Houston is a city that should've never been created, at least in its current location. Many have said Houston is built on a swamp, or, in modern terminology, a floodplain!

Every community has an essence or that which makes it what it is, a personality if you will. Houston is a blue-collar town. Here, people work with their hands. We make things, find things, transform things, move things, and heal people. Don't get me wrong. There's a lot of intellectual property created and *used* here. But, that isn't the essence of Houston. If you want a place that thinks and theorizes for a living, visit Austin. **Houston gets things done.**

Houston is the energy capital of the world. The 3,700+ energy-related enterprises headquartered in Houston and the people who work within those enterprises, do some of the most dangerous, dirty and strenuous work in the world. These organizations and their people find and produce oil and gas, refine and transform that oil and gas into essential products, and move those products all over the world.

Houston has the largest and one of the best, perhaps **the** best, medical centers in the world. People from all over the world come here for healing. Here, doctors, nurses and hundreds of other medical professionals work with their hands helping others find health and life. This is also a dangerous and dirty business requiring great mental and physical stamina. Spend a few days near the operating theaters at Houston Methodist Hospital or the Baylor St. Luke's Medical Center, and you'll see what I mean.

Perhaps, then, it's a bit easier to understand Houston's response to the devastation of hurricane Harvey. A people accustomed to acting, doing and getting their hands dirty, got their boats, canoes, kayaks, trucks and whatever else that was useful and rushed headlong into danger helping their fellow humans. No one had to tell Houstonians to act. It's part of our community DNA. Houstonians not only get things done, but we share a lot of other community attributes. Here are a few of them.

Houston Ship Channel

The following applies to the Houston Metropolitan Area, which consists of nine counties with a land mass of 10,062 square miles and, according to a 2017 estimate, was home to 6.9 million people. The highest elevation is 430 feet, and the lowest is sea level, which **may** have contributed to a bit of hurricane Harvey flooding. Here are a few of Houston's attributes.

- *The Houston Astros are the 2017 World Series Champions!*
- *Houston is the most ethnically diverse metropolis in the country.*
- *Houston is the third-largest city in the U.S. and home to 54 Fortune 500 companies, second only to New York City's 55.*
- *At last count, there were more than 140 languages spoken in Houston.*
- *More than 150 museums and cultural institutions contribute to Houston's unique social mosaic, including more than 14 institutions of higher learning.*

Texas Medical Center in Houston

- Houstonians love to eat out, as demonstrated by more than 10,000 eating establishments serving more than 60 different cuisines.
- Houston is the energy capital of the world. Over 3,700 Houston-based establishments serve the industry. Houston accounts for 40% of our nation's base petrochemical capacity.
- Houston is the third-most humid city in the country, receiving an average of 49 inches of rain per year. Hurricane Harvey dumped that much in five days!
- Houston's deep-water port is first in the United States in international waterborne tonnage handled. The port is the 10th largest in the world.
- Houston's Theatre District's concentration of venue-seats is second only to New York City.
- Houston is equidistant from both the East and West Coasts. It is 1,630 miles to New York and 1,560 miles to Los Angeles. You can reach any metro area within hours by air.
- Houston is home to the NASA Johnson Space Center, the epicenter of the United States' space program. More than a million people visit the Space Center every year.
- The Houston Livestock Show and Rodeo is the largest in the world and has over 2.3 million visitors per year.

- *Houston is home to the Texas Medical Center. It is the largest in the world, hosting more than 4.8 million patient-visits a year.*

THE HOME INVADER WHO REFUSED TO LEAVE

Hurricane Harvey As Viewed from Space

Unlike most hurricanes that deliver a massive storm surge, blow hard and move on, Harvey was special. It brought storm surge and high winds to Rockport, Texas where it made landfall. The storm then made its way to the Houston Metropolitan Area and stayed and stayed and stayed.

- *Made landfall on August 25, 2017 at Rockport, Texas*
- *First Category 4 hurricane to strike United States mainland since 2005.*
- *130 mph sustained winds at landfall.*
- *Dumped nearly four feet of rain on the Houston Metropolitan area.*

- *Caused an estimated $125 billion in property damage, tied with hurricane Katrina*
- *Destroyed or damaged over 260,000 homes and businesses.*
- *Killed more than 80 people.*
- *Destroyed an estimated one million cars.*
- *Devastated the lives of more than 450,000 people.*
- *Was so destructive, its name has been retired from the pool of future hurricane names!*
- **Brought a community together like never before.**
- **Showed us all what ethical intelligence looks like in action!**

Hurricane Harvey also left us with a couple of artifacts or souvenirs, if you will—Harvey "Water" and Harvey "Brain."

Harvey Water aka "The Water"

Hurricane Harvey Flood Water in Houston

INTRODUCTION

"Water, water, everywhere, and all the boards did shrink; Water, water, everywhere, Nor any drop to drink." This verse, taken from Coleridge's *The Rime of the Ancient Mariner*, expresses a sailor's lament of being surrounded by undrinkable water. The verse also captures a memory mosaic shared by all of us who lived through the aquatic "adventure" known as hurricane Harvey.

> "Water, water, everywhere, And all the boards did shrink; Water, water, everywhere, Nor any drop to drink."

As I write this, the unusual Houston winter of 2018, is nearly over—it snowed three times! We're also marking the six-month anniversary of hurricane Harvey rude interruption of our 2017 blast-furnace summer. During the past six months, I've formally interviewed dozens of people, held semiformal discussions with hundreds of others and casually discussed Harvey with too many more to count. Then, suddenly, I had an epiphany!

It happened a few days ago. I was wrapping up an interview with Scott Crowder, news anchor with KTRH NewsRadio in Houston. He was punctuating his commentary with the phrase, "the water, "the water," the water." Then, it hit me! We're obsessed with "The Water!" I'd heard this phrase frequently repeated in every Harvey-related discussion I'd had since Harvey.

> Harvey's flood water flowed everywhere, into and out of sewers, junk yards, plant sites, medical waste pits, bayous, drainage ditches and over thousands of miles of streets and parking lots.

My realization was so sharp and unexpected that I interrupted Scott with, "WOW! You've just caused me to realize something profound!" Scott was pleased, and I was grateful. Let's explore this phenomenon, some might even call it a phobia—Harvey Water!

We all know what water is, right? It's H_2O, two hydrogen atoms bound to one oxygen atom. These days, we have all kinds of water. We have plain water, light water, heavy water and "healthy" water, just to name a few. Plain water is, well, just plain water. Light water is known as such only when used to cool a light-water nuclear reactor. Heavy water is a hydrogen isotope deuterium bound to oxygen instead of hydrogen. I think you get the water diversity picture.

Humans have a love-hate relationship with water. We love water because it provides us with many benefits, a cold drink on a hot day, a hot cleansing shower or bath, an enjoyable day boating or fishing and beautiful views and soothing sounds on a beach. We also love water because it's vital to our life—about 60% of our body consists of water. We can't live without it!

Humans hate water because of its destructive power. Water erodes beaches and can stain whatever it touches. Water washes away topsoil and, when frozen, makes traveling treacherous. Six inches of fast-moving water can move a two-ton vehicle! Finally, the leading cause of death from worldwide natural disasters is flooding. Hurricane Harvey's flooding literally brought these dangers into our homes and figuratively burned them into our psyches.

Harvey's flood water flowed everywhere, into and out of sewers, junk yards, plant sites, medical waste pits, bayous, drainage ditches and over thousands of miles of streets and parking lots. During its journey from its source to the Gulf of Mexico, this water became a toxic soup of hazardous chemicals, infectious bacteria, dangerous viruses, venomous snakes, angry fire ants and flowing electricity, just to name a few of the ingredients.

"The water" corrupted everything it touched. "The water" leveled fences, moved buildings, swept people off their feet and destroyed thousands of vehicles. One survivor I interviewed said the water was the one thing she feared most. "It was dark, nasty, smelly, and contained floating human excrement." One civilian rescuer said, "Walking in that water was the scariest part of our work. Not knowing what was in the water that we couldn't see was the worst part of the experience."

If you talk to someone who was there and ask them about "the water", you get a facial/body language and an oral response as though you had just asked for the secret society handshake! Perhaps, we can call it the not-so-secret Harvey Water Society because we all know that with hurricane Harvey, it wasn't the wind. It was "the water"—Harvey Water, which may have contributed to a condition called Harvey Brain!

> Wear it as your badge of #Houston Strong pride, or your Texan "badassness"! Go Astros! Go Dynamo! Go Rockets! Go Texans!

Harvey Brain AKA "The Moment"

HURRICANE HARVEY, HOUSTON AND HEROISM

If you were in the Houston Metropolitan Area during the hurricane and Biblical flood known as Harvey, and you experienced one or more of the following:

- Harvey Water **surrounding** your home.
- Harvey Water **in** your home.
- A forced boat, truck or helicopter ride out of your neighborhood.
- The smell of chlorine bleach in the morning, **every** morning.
- An unwanted foray into dirty, smelly or polluted water, aka Harvey Water.
- A car with watermarks on the dashboard.
- The joy of having a completely new wardrobe.
- The delight of seeing all your stuff piled high on the curb.
- Flooded streets, power outages or unscheduled vacation time.
- Celebrated Christmas 2017, using paper plates and plastic stemware.
- Became a volunteer helping strangers.
- The privilege of having a house payment **and** an apartment rent payment.
- Have friends or family members who experienced any of these.

Then, you've most likely experienced "the moment," a newly diagnosed condition called *Harvey Brain*. This phenomenon was first isolated and identified by Dr. Kevin Bohacs, a senior research geologist at ExxonMobil who diagnosed his friend Cindy Yeilding, another insightful geologist turned corporate executive at BP America. Kevin assured his friend Cindy, that she "was not alone in her mental fuzziness." He went on to say, "The condition is common after such incidents and it's good that people will realize that they are not being made fun of but share their challenges with all around them."

Thank you, Cindy and Kevin. Your names will be forever linked to *fuzzy* thinking! ☺

So, what exactly is Harvey Brain?

Harvey Brain is a mental state that can descend upon Harvey Survivors without any notice. It can manifest as a wet mental blanket, as depicted in the photograph, often accompanied by the aforementioned "mental fuzziness." Or, it can show up, often accompanied by a blank stare, as a momentary time shift back to that dreadful ten days and a reliving of the experience. Or, as in my case, remembering being surrounded by multiple feet of water **but** the water **not** entering your home by inches, a memory often accompanied by tears of gratitude. Or, it can manifest as a remembrance of the heavy sorrow in the air as people were suffering.

We should remember, the empaths among us suffer this malady more acutely than the general population. If you know any, be Houston-kind. So, what can you do about it? Not much!

WEAR IT AS YOUR BADGE OF #HOUSTONSTRONG PRIDE, OR YOUR TEXAN BADASSNESS"!
GO ASTROS! GO DYNAMO! GO ROCKETS! GO TEXANS!

READ ABOUT OUR UNSUNG HEROES! VISIT THE HARVEY HEROES AKA "THE UNSUNG" SECTION AT THE BACK OF THE BOOK

CELEBRATING THE COMPASSION, CARING, AND

CHAPTER 1

BREATHING GOODNESS

View from My (Author's) Garage Early Morning, Monday August 28, 2017

Like most Houstonians who lived through hurricane Ike in 2008, Linda, my wife of 32 years, and I monitor tropical activity closely during hurricane season. So, we began watching hurricane Harvey form shortly after it emerged into the Gulf of Mexico, after passing over the Yucatán Peninsula. When the storm began heading in our direction, we started making the typical hurricane/tropical storm preparations, stocking up on bottled water, batteries, and non-perishable food.

We live in a subdivision that is about 13 years old. It was built on the grounds of an old working farm, and we live next door to the old farmhouse, which has since been converted into an extended care, hospice-like facility. Our subdivision is surrounded by other neighborhoods that are more than 30 years old. There is a man-made lake in the middle of our subdivision, and we live next to it, one of the reasons we bought our home as it was being built in 2005.

The lake is fed by natural underground springs and a drainage system designed to catch the backyard rain runoff from most of the homes in our neighborhood. The normal level of the lake is approximately 15 feet below the bank. The amount of water in the lake varies with rainfall, and it's only been full one time. And, that was due to an unusual 2016 rainstorm that dropped 22 inches of water in less than 12 hours.

Our lot is the highest point in our neighborhood, probably because it's located next to the old farmhouse. According to official floodplain maps, we live in a 1000-year flooding location, which means the chance of our home flooding in any given year is one tenth of one percent. As a result, we weren't required to purchase flood insurance, and we never had.

I wasn't worried about my house flooding. It never had, and based on the best engineering information available, it never would, unless I lived as long as Methuselah. So, I wasn't flippant, but I wasn't particularly worried either.

> I wasn't worried about my house flooding. It never had, and based on the best engineering information available, it never would, unless I lived as long as Methuselah.

Besides, we'd lived through 12 hours of 80 mile-per-hour winds and driving rain as hurricane Ike passed through our neighborhood in 2008. We had a lot of wind damage in our neighborhood, but little flooding. Our windows were boarded over during Ike. So, we couldn't see our yard until the wind quit blowing. But, when we emerged from the house, the level of the lake was high but nowhere near leaving its banks. And, there was no flooding on our street. We were high and dry, and I was able to drive out of the neighborhood immediately following the hurricane!

As hurricane Harvey moved north in the Gulf of Mexico, weather forecasters were convinced it would come ashore southwest of Houston. For the Greater Houston Metropolitan area, they were forecasting a significant "rain event", but that was it. Linda and I both remembered living unscathed through both hurricane Ike and the fluke 22-inch-12-hour rainstorm in the spring of 2016. So, we were optimistic about the minimal effect the storm would have on us. So optimistic that we glossed over the local news outlets reporting the factoid that more than one million new people had moved to the Greater Houston Area since hurricane Ike hit in 2008.

Ducks in Author's Cul-de-Sac

Although hurricane Harvey didn't make landfall until Friday evening the 25th, it started raining at our house Thursday afternoon. The rain didn't stop until the following Wednesday morning. All day Friday it rained hard at times, more slowly at others. We watched the hurricane make landfall on Friday night, taking greatest amusement from watching national TV correspondents being blown to the ground by the high wind. The rain outside became heavier, and it rained heavily all-night long.

The rain continued all day Saturday, and the lake had filled up to within a few feet of the top of its banks. Although my backyard contained around 3 inches of water, it was draining steadily. And, there was no street flooding. The rain continued all during the night. Even early Sunday morning, our street was only under about six inches of water, as illustrated by the nearby photo showing ducks swimming in our cul-de-sac. Other parts of Houston were not faring as well.

The downtown area was under several feet of water, and many famous local landmarks were flooded, including several major arts venues. During Sunday afternoon, the water drained out of our street, and I decided to make a last-minute visit to the only open store in our neighborhood. While I was in the store, the rain started coming down in sheets again, and in my hurry to return home, I backed into a nearly invisible post in the parking lot, knocking out my taillight—$1,700 worth of damage! We used to have real bumpers on cars, but that's another story.

My (Author's) Street

When I got home, I relayed my sad story to Linda. Without missing a beat, she said, "I told you not to go out! Where's the stuff you went out to get?" Through my angry and gritted teeth, I retorted "They were out of it!" There was a long silence. Suddenly, Linda broke out into uncontrollable laughter. Not seeing the humor in such a dark episode, I went to my home office to sulk.

The driving rain that had started during my unfortunate trip to the store, became more intense and continued throughout the night. Before going to bed, I checked our street, and it was still clear. At five in the morning, Monday, August 28th, one of our beloved furry creatures decided he had to go outside and take care of some "business." When I opened the door, he saw how hard it was raining and decided that he could "hold" it for a while.

While walking back to our bedroom, I glanced out my front door. I thought I saw the streetlight reflecting off some waves in my front yard! As we have a large-beveled glass front door, I thought it surely must be an optical illusion because of the curved glass. So, I opened the door to look out and was astonished to see water lapping up against my sidewalk, about three feet from my porch. In a short few hours our street had become totally impassable under feet of water.

I was becoming alarmed at a quickening rate. And, since it was my normal schedule to get up anyway, I decided it was time to get my high-powered flashlight and check all our doors, windows and yard. I first went out my back door. My backyard was underwater, which is not that unusual during heavy rain.

Author And Dog Rocky

Then, I noticed the nursing center's lights were out. It seemed they had evacuated all the residents while I slept. This had never happened before! I immediately concluded the nursing home staff knew something I didn't. Nervously, I went to check the front of the house.

My Prayer Warrior

When I opened my garage door, I nearly fell over when I saw water within three feet of the door. I quickly placed my flashlight beam on the surface of the water and traced the water out towards the lake. There wasn't a break in the water! The lake had overflowed and was spilling into our cul-de-sac! This had never happened!

It was at this point that I knew we were in big trouble! I returned to the kitchen and started a pot of coffee. I went into the bedroom to put on some clothes and told my sleeping wife, "Baby, I think we're in trouble." Linda is a late-night person. So, at five in the morning, she's only been in bed a few hours and dead to the world. In a grouchy/sleepy voice, she said, "Should we pack up and leave?" I said, "That's the trouble. I don't think we can!" She said, "Well if that's the case, I'll just sleep some more."

Miffed that she wasn't taking the danger I perceived seriously, I returned to the kitchen for my first 20-ounce-cup of coffee. I went to watch the water rising towards my garage. At daybreak, I could clearly see how much conditions had deteriorated while it was dark. I looked out over my neighborhood and couldn't see dryland, as shown in the nearby picture of an airboat rescuing people. We were surrounded by multiple **feet** of water. With-

Air Boats In Author's Neighborhood

out a boat, we couldn't leave, even if we wanted to. And, I didn't have a boat. With Rocky, my best dog-friend, shown in a previous picture, sitting at my side, we watched the wind-driven rain continue and the water slowly creeping up my driveway.

After about an hour, Linda joined us in the garage. Together watching the rain and the rising water, we felt helpless. Remembering an old Christian admonition, "When you don't know what else to say, just say the name of Jesus." We joined hands and started praying for the rain to stop. After our prayer, we embraced and started weeping. It looked like our home was about to be destroyed by the flood water. At times like that, interesting factoid thoughts come to mind. In my case, one was, *We just installed this new floor!*

Author's Neighborhood Rescue

My mind jerked back to the moment because the power flashed out. Linda began texting our other family members. None of them were in danger of flooding. But, our daughter was determined to find a way to rescue us. It wasn't until we texted her a picture of first responders in National Guard trucks and airboats rescuing people across the lake from us that she abandoned any thoughts of rescue attempts. Then, we heard the helicopters! The water had risen to almost nine feet in the homes in the neighborhood behind ours, and people were being rescued from rooftops, which is shown in a nearby photo. We were trapped!

I stood in my garage watching the rain and the rising water.

Three houses down the street from us had already been flooded by 2-3 feet of water. A national guard truck had rescued the occupants. Our neighbor texted and invited us and our two dogs to join them on the second floor of their home. They knew our only move could have been to the attic. Fortunately, we had an ax! My neighbor across the cul-de-sac yelled,

"Are you leaving?" I yelled back,

"No! We're staying." He motioned they were staying too.

After a while longer, I wondered where Linda had gone. I went looking and found her standing at the front of our house looking out the window at the rising water. She was praying out loud, forbidding the water to come any further! And, she was humming the tune of Darlene Zschech's *In Jesus Name* that we regularly sing in church.

Some of the lyrics are, *God is fighting for us. Pushing back the darkness. Lighting up the kingdom. We will not be shaken.* That song had become her survival battle hymn in 2015 while recovering from life-threatening surgery. I thought, *Wow! I've been living with a prayer-warrior all these years and didn't know it!*

> *I thought, Wow! I've been living with a prayer-warrior all these years and didn't know it!*

Me? I returned to the garage and noted the water had risen further. Like most men, I began brainstorming about what to **do in this realm**. There was a problem to solve! I began elevating furniture using bricks. I moved boxes of books from the garage into the house. After about an hour of heavy labor, all without the benefit of air conditioning, I was hot, sweaty and realized the futility of my effort.

Being the great man of faith I am, I started mentally questioning God. *God why is this happening to me? I live a righteous life! I tithe my income! I help others whenever I can! I don't lie, cheat or steal!* No answers came.

After my faith-questioning session, I noticed the rain was coming down harder and the water was still rising. I continued posting pictures on Facebook soliciting prayers and intercessions. One of my high school classmates suggested sandbags.

Ah ha! Who knew I would need sandbags! A boat would've been a better option.

I went searching for Linda again. I found her exactly where I'd left

My (Author's) Neighborhood.

her—praying! She stood in that window singing and praying until the water stopped rising at around mid-afternoon. It was within a few inches of our garage door! Proverbs tells us the "Prayers of a righteous woman availeth much."

That passage was manifest that day! Of the houses on our street, all but ours, the house next door, and the house across the cul-de-sac, flooded that day. The remainder of the homes suffered varying degrees of damage. And, as I write this chapter, piles of debris from those damaged homes still line the streets of my neighborhood, as noted in the nearby photo.

You might recall my great acts of faith and courage as I questioned God a few pages back, complaining about my suffering, more like inconvenience, and wondering *why me?* A few days later as I was investigating the immense damage to my neighborhood, out of the blue came the answer— "I spared your home so that you could tell the world about Houston's human goodness."

This book is my response!

Although I personally lived through that awful flooding experience, it was only "my" experience. So, I immersed myself in the experience of others by walking through devastated neighborhoods feeling the sorrow, pain and hope present in the piles of rubble outside each home. I listened to and experienced stories of faith, courage, self-sacrifice, decency, and goodness. I also walked among and talked to survivors of this life-changing tragedy. I visited one of Houston's busiest rescue centers.

A Soul-Etching Visit

Until that day in late August, I'd never visited a rescue center of any kind. So, I went to the George R. Brown Convention Center in downtown Houston where the city of Houston had established a large rescue operation. Ironically, my visit occurred a few days after the rain had stopped. It was a beautiful sunshine-filled-day-with-moderate-temperatures outside the convention center. Inside, not so much.

The Security. Because of the lawlessness that took place in the New Orleans Superdome after Katrina, I expected a heavy security presence. The security I encountered exceeded even my highest expectations. Areas outside the convention center were heavily patrolled by a variety of law enforcement agencies. Entry into the convention center was closely monitored by officers from the Houston Police Department.

Upon arrival, a nice, polite but business-like-latex-glove-wearing police officer informed me that only registered survivors with wristbands and people with prior written authorization were allowed into the convention center. I explained that I was a local writer, and that I was writing a book about Houston and hurricane Harvey. She asked what that had to do with the convention center. I explained that I needed to walk around inside the convention center (pictured nearby) talking to people, hearing and feeling what they were experiencing so that my book would be realistic.

She said, "You're going to have to talk to my supervisor."

So, she stuck her head in the door and yelled, "Sarge I need you over here!"

George R. Brown Convention Center

After a few minutes, another nice, polite but business-like-latex-glove-wearing police officer came out to talk to me. I gave him the same explanation I had provided to the previous police officer. He said,

"That sounds okay to me, but you need Red Cross approval." I asked,

"How do I get that?" He said,

"Let me go talk to the Red Cross person in charge for you. But, they're going to insist that you have an escort." I said,

About half of the people coming to the door were looking to volunteer. They were told there was no need because the volunteer requirement had been met early in the morning.

"That's okay with me." The sergeant left. I stood marveling at the continuous activity at the door. The stream of people seeking admittance never stopped. About half of the people coming to the door were seeking to volunteer. They were told there was no need because the volunteer requirement had been met early in the morning. Others looking for help were told to go to NRG Stadium, the other large rescue center because

Inside George R. Brown Convention Center

no more survivors were being accepted at this site.

About 20 minutes later—it seemed like an hour—the supervisor returned and said,

"You're all set. They aren't requiring an escort for you. If you need anything just talk to the people at that desk over there."

I stepped inside and immediately encountered a pat-down-personal-body-search by another police officer. He explained that everyone coming into the convention center was subject to a firearm and contraband search. After the search, and again after explaining my reason for visiting the convention center, I was free to go about my research.

During my visit, I saw Department of Homeland Security personnel, National Guard service members, Harris County sheriffs and constables, and the ever-present Houston Police Department.

The Place. As one might imagine, a premier "business" convention center, as shown in the previous picture, was orderly, clean and businesslike. The hallways looked a lot like they might appear during any kind of business conference. Vendors and other organizations had set up booths offering their products and/or services. My first thought was, *Wow, this looks a lot like the hundreds of conventions and conferences I had attended during my career.* Then, I realized the level of security present.

Again, my thoughts returned to the security problems experienced in the aftermath of hurricane Katrina in New Orleans in 2005. The city of Houston also hosted some Katrina survivors in the old Astrodome. I recall there were also security lapses in that facility. Well, that wasn't the case in this rescue center.

Everywhere I went, I encountered heavy security. During my visit, I saw Department of Homeland Security personnel, National Guard service members, Harris County sheriffs and constables, and the ever-present Houston Police Department. In fact, it seemed like the entire police department was present in the convention center. So, when I say security was tight—it was tight! Even to the point of intimidation. But, I'd rather be a bit intimidated than mugged!

Inside George R. Brown Convention Center

I walked the hallways first, talking to quite a variety of people but mostly vendor representatives. The cell phone companies were well represented, and there were a few financial institutions. The city of Houston had a large presence, and there were other social services agencies available, including a couple of churches. I noticed few survivors visiting the service providers. The atmosphere seemed formal, businesslike AND sterile.

The Battlefield. I entered the large public hall, a truly cavernous concrete and steel structure with, 35-foot ceilings. This space was the commons area where everyone came for food, relaxation and recreation and general fellowship, as shown in the nearby photo. With the high ceilings and the concrete floor, sounds ricocheted everywhere. The din was palpable, making it difficult to hold private conversations.

The other halls were dedicated to sleeping and personal care. Entry into those spaces was guarded by polite but firm National Guard personnel. I was told that only people who wore survivor wristbands were allowed into those areas. It seemed like an appropriate security precaution, which is what I told the two large uniformed men blocking my path.

The hall was laid out into several roped or screened-off subareas each with its own function. There was an entertainment subarea with a Jumbotron-like screen that was showing local television programs. The space included a children's play subarea replete with playground equipment. It was eerily empty of children. Another subarea was fenced off for Walmart. I was told that Walmart was providing toiletries, paper towels, and other similar personal hygiene items. That subarea was busy.

The largest subarea was set up with tables and chairs. Large round tables could seat up to 10 - 12 people. Most of the tables were picnic table-sized and surrounded by folding chairs. I was

CHAPTER 1: BREATHING GOODNESS

there after lunch, so the area was only about 50% occupied by folks who had just received a ration of paper towels, toilet paper, and personal hygiene items.

As I walked around, stopping frequently to talk to people, I felt engulfed by deep pervading sorrow, dark fear and rebellious resignation bordering on anger. I felt like a dark wet invisible blanket had enveloped me. The sorrow hung like a foul smell. The fear and anger in the air almost made me paranoid for my safety. There was no banter one might expect in such a large gathering of people. In fact, there was scant survivor conversation.

> I felt like a dark wet invisible blanket had enveloped me. The sorrow hung like a foul smell. The fear and anger in the air almost made me paranoid for my safety.

It was like I had walked onto a spent battlefield where the debris had been airbrushed out of the scene. But the people were still there. You could almost see ephemeral figments of the flooded cars, destroyed dwellings and floating memories of photos, clothing and knick-knacks. People were silently staring into space or their electronic devices. They had extinguished the outside world. These were fragile hurting people, as depicted in the nearby photo. Under different circumstance, one of them could have been me.

The Survivors. The survivors I approached were polite and receptive to my presence, especially after I told them I was a *local* writer and had also experienced the flooding. They seemed pleased that

Distraught Harvey Survivor

someone was taking a **personal** interest in what had happened to them and genuinely interested in hearing their stories. Nonetheless, three out of four declined to talk about their experience. At first, I wasn't sure why there was a disconnect between their approachability and their desire to tell me their story. After a few conversations with those who would talk to me, the reason for the disconnect became clear.

For the most part, these people were suffering from various stages of shock, perhaps even some level of PTSD. They didn't want to talk about their experience because talking about it meant reliving it in their minds. Our minds are like instant replay cameras. When the brain stores memories, it stores all aspects of that memory including sights, sounds and especially smells. In fact, some neuroscientists, believe that memory recall is cataloged based on smell, which is why a whiff of perfume or cologne can instantly remind us of someone who is a distant memory.

As I mentioned, I've never been in a rescue shelter—unless we consider a snow-storm-induced overnight stay with friends in a gymnasium after a high school basketball game "rescue shelter" experience! After a few days, living in a rescue shelter is a boring and monotonous experience. You have lots of time on your hands, and an idle mind engages in all types of imagining and worrying. You relive your traumatic experience many times, and your mind produces thousands of unpleasant alternative scenarios that induce more sorrow, worry and fear for the future. Here is one of those stories.

Lori's Story. Although I recorded and transcribed this interview, most of the "direct quotations" that you see have been edited. This is a traumatic story. I'm thankful that Lori was able to relate it to me. But, as you can imagine, it was a tearful conversation punctuated with lapses and repeated comments. So, what you see, is an edited version of her story.

Me: What part of the area are you from?
Lori: The Cypress area. Cypress Station, I-45 and 1960
Me: That's not far from me. How were you rescued?
Lori: By boat. They brought us out on a boat.
Me: How long did you wait to be rescued?
Lori: Three days.
Me: Three days?!
Lori: Three long days! I waited three days for them to rescue me. I went out on social media seeking out help. So, people in the boats and the people in big dumpster trucks were coming to rescue people out of our neighborhood and out of our apartment complex.

I waited three long days. Me and my five kids and my husband. We waited three long days.

Me: Did you have water in your home the whole time?

Lori: Yes. And, on the third day a tornado came down I-45.

Me: How did you know there was a tornado?

Lori: They were warning the public by beating on our door... told us we had to get out. We had to military evacuate. Now once the police told us we had to military evacuate, then I opened my door. The water came rushing in.

I had a townhouse. So, all that water rushing into my house... Then, we heard the tornado warning sirens. We thought we were all gonna die!

The EMS people yelled for us to take cover. We heard the wind blowin' real hard. I shut my door. We ran through the water for the bathroom, and we laid in the tub.

> The tornado popped out the windows in our apartment! It popped out the windows!! It started sucking the roof off my house!!

The tornado popped out the windows in our apartment! It popped out the windows!! It started sucking the roof off my house!! It started sucking the roof up, and my kids were in the bathroom!! We stayed there! It passed over us.

Me: What happened after the tornado passed over?

Lori: We left the house.

Me: How deep was the water?

Lori: Up to here.

Me: Up to your chin?

> Yes! The water was up to my chin! My kids were in a boat. We walked almost a mile in the water to get out. We left so fast, we brought nothing with us. No clothes. No phone. No identification. Nothing!

Lori: Yes! The water was up to my chin! My kids were in a boat. We walked almost a mile in the water to get out. We left so fast, we brought nothing with us. No clothes. No phone. No identification. Nothing!

Me: No identification?

Lori: No. Nothing!

Me: How did you get here?

Lori: Coast Guard helicopter. We walked in the water to a big National Guard truck. It took us to a high place. Then the helicopter.

Me: How did you get in here?

Lori: They just let everyone in. We didn't have any ID, but they just let us in.

Me: When did you know you were going to have to leave your house?

Lori: I knew I was gonna have to leave Friday because the water was already rising. But they didn't rescue us until Sunday. I kept calling the rescue people, but the line was so busy. I kept calling 911, but I was told to stop calling 911 because it was reserved for the people that really had an emergency. They said they were trying to get to us. They were telling us to be patient and wait on the rescue people to come. But it was, like, they ain't coming. We waited Friday, Saturday and Sunday. They didn't come rescue us 'til Sunday night.

Me: How'd you know they were coming? Did they call you?

Lori: How did we know? We didn't know, we walked in water... we walked in water and we waited.

Me: So you had water in your house?

Lori: I had water in my house the whole time. We moved to the second floor. The police beat on the door. And they had people in the boats beating at the door making sure nobody wasn't in there...but we were on the second floor. We had a power outage. All the water was on the first floor already.

Me: So, you couldn't hear the beating on the door?

Lori: No

Me: What was your darkest hour?

Lori: Walking in that water!

Me: The walk in the water?

Lori: Yes, the walk in the water and not knowing what was in that water. We were so scared of that water. We didn't know what was in the water.

Me: Could you see anything in the water?

Lori: It was so dirty, brown and nasty. There was bathroom stuff floating in the water!! It was up to my chin...and the brown nasty stuff was everywhere.

Me: There were feces floating in the water?

Lori: Yes. Turds in the water!! But my darkest was when we ran out of food. We ran out of water. We ran out of baby drinks. I have five babies under the age of six. My oldest one is six. So, when they couldn't eat, I knew it was time to get out of there. I knew it was time to go but, we didn't have nowhere to go. We were so scared of that water. We didn't know what was in that water.

Me: So, what was going on in your neighborhood?

Lori: People were coming to rescue family members by boat. They had family support. We were all alone.

Me: How about your neighbors? Did they all make it out.

Lori: No. The lady next door passed away. They [National Guard] took us back to get our things. There was nothing to get. Nothing was left. It had all floated away. I asked if they had checked next door. They said no. They went and forced opened the door. They found her dead inside.

Me: What has been the worst part for you?

Lori: The worst part is when you lose everything, and you can't get it back.

Me: Did you have flood insurance?

Lori: No.

Me: I don't have flood insurance either. It's never flooded.

Lori: Exactly. I had apartment insurance. But, that doesn't help.

Me: What's next?

Lori: We have to start all over. We have nothing! I have a job, but I can't get there. My husband has a job, but he can't get there. Our cars are gone. We have an apartment for four months through FEMA. It's so hard...

Me: You're alive.

Lori: Yes, and my five kids and husband. We have to start over. It's so hard.....

> They both had jobs and worked hard. Yet, in a moment, circumstances beyond their control uprooted that stake and washed away everything they had built.

This was a difficult talk. For most of the conversation, tears were streaming down Lori's face. Because of my near-flooding experience, I deeply felt her sorrow and despair and was holding my own tears back. It's a tragic story. Here was a young couple driving a stake into the ground determined to lay a claim to the American dream for themselves and their children. They both had jobs and worked hard. Yet, in a moment, circumstances beyond their control uprooted that stake and washed away everything they had built.

It may have been more dramatic, but Lori's experience was but one of hundreds of stories living in hearts and minds of those in the rescue center that day. Despite the temporarily voided lives I encountered, I sensed hope leavened with stoicism, sadness tempered with determination, and gratitude shaded with a bit of cynicism. And, I prayed the anger I sensed would subside with time.

Anger is a natural reaction to death. All the people residing in the rescue center that day were alive physically, some barely escaping physical death. But, they were dealing with tragedies resembling death. For many, a dream had died. For others, a way of life had passed away. Whatever the reason for the death perception, these survivors were passing through some stage of grief.

Elisabeth Kubler-Ross created a model addressing the grief associated with death. In this model, she suggested five stages of grief—denial, anger, bargaining, depression and acceptance. Every survivor in that rescue center was passing through these stages, some more rapidly than others. Perhaps, we should pay more attention to helping survivors deal with their grief.

Here are some random comments I left the rescue center with, "My life has been wiped." Or, "I've been reduced to nothing." Or, "I'm in God's hands." Or, "I'm so happy you're writing a book about this. People need to remember what happened to us."

Volunteers Serving First Responders

My commitment is, we *will* remember what happened to us and how we responded to it! I left the convention center that day a jumble of emotions but more determined than ever to write this story—the Houston story that could change the world.

Houston's Gift

Hurricane Harvey came to harm and destroy, and that it did. Hurricane Harvey and its aftermath has become one of the worst Texas natural disasters ever. Despite the devastation, the people of Houston used the occasion to give the world a priceless gift. In our response to this tragedy, **we showed the goodness that is at the core of our humanity**, as depicted in the nearby picture of volunteers serving first responders.

In today's world, we don't see this often. Most of the time that goodness lies dormant and hidden in our consciousness, manifesting only rarely during times of distress, crisis and tragedy.

For more than a decade, I've had the privilege and joy of studying, researching and writing about this phenomenon. This special gift that lies at our human core is not a new discovery. It's as old as we are, however old humans are. The oldest written evidence I've found of this phenomenon is etched into the physical structure we know as the great pyramid at Giza, or about 5,000 years old.

> Despite the devastation, the people of Houston used the occasion to give the world a priceless gift. In our response to this tragedy, **we showed the goodness that is at the core of our humanity** ...

This phenomenon is discussed in the writings of all major religions, faith and spiritual traditions. Confucius referred to it as *Ren* or humaneness. Socrates gave it the name *hē en tōi* ēthei *noē-*

sis, and Aristotle embraced it as *phronesis* or practical wisdom. Augustine and other Christian scholars studied it as prudence. We now know this manifest goodness as human ethical intelligence.

Ethical Intelligence. Ethical intelligence is the engine powering our behavior. During those five fateful fall days, while hurricane Harvey tormented Southeast Texas, we showed the world what a fully-developed adult ethical intelligence looks like in action. We put aside our differences. We placed the welfare of others ahead of ourselves, some even to the point of risking their lives. We freely shared our material possessions. We felt the pain of others. We cried with and for others.

We didn't categorize one another. We didn't see skin color or ethnicity. Rescuers didn't ask if you were straight, lesbian, gay, bi, or trans. If you needed help, someone helped! We saw one another clearly as equal fellow humans, an important aspect of adult ethical intelligence. Goodness was in the air. We took joy in breathing it in. Our attitude was, "We could get used to this!"

> We didn't categorize one another. We didn't see skin color or ethnicity. Rescuers didn't ask if you were straight, lesbian, gay, bi, or trans. If you needed help, someone helped!

I'm pleased to tell you, it's possible!

That grand gift that normally lies dormant in our consciousness became fully visible in our human relationships during those days. For those five days most of us put aside our normally withered childish ethical intelligence. Instead, we displayed the fully-developed adult version all of us are capable of. It's as simple as that!

Being good to one another is the outward expression of a fully-developed adult ethical intelligence. Here is a metaphor that makes this idea easier to understand. A motor vehicle is powered by its engine. We see the outward expression of that unseen engine as vehicle movement. The car doesn't move by itself. The engine powers the movement that we see. We know it's there, and, if we opened the engine compartment, we could verify, "Yep, the engine's in there!"

Similarly, our behavior has an engine. We see evidence of it by looking at how we act in our human relationships. Here are some examples. I respect my wife. Or, I flip you off or honk my horn when you cut me off in traffic. Or, I invest time in my children. Or, I watch pornographic videos on my job instead of working. Or, I take ownership of mistakes my team members make. The list is endless.

Just like the engine in our car moves the car, our ethical intelligence moves our behavior. A gasoline or diesel engine moves our car because of thousands of fuel-air-mixture explosions per minute. Our ethical intelligence moves our behavior because of thousands of ethical judgments per hour. We understand the essence of an internal combustion engine is combustion. Similarly, we understand the essence of ethical intelligence is ethical judging.

Unfortunately, at this point our metaphor breaks down because we can successfully drive a motor vehicle without understanding how the engine and its internal components work. We can't do that with ethical intelligence. We can't achieve a fully-developed adult ethical intelligence without understanding its moving parts and how they fit together.

To perfectly operate a motor vehicle, we don't need to know about the crankshaft, the pistons, the connecting rods or the valves or how those components operate together. For us to exercise a fully-developed adult ethical intelligence, however; we must know about our worldview window, internal compass, ethical fence and our comfort zone and how these parts work together.

The good news is we aren't going to study such matters in this book! I've created a growing body of material on ethical intelligence. For those who are interested in obtaining a deeper understanding of the engine that is ethical intelligence, consult my website and Amazon and other bookstores. Our purpose in this book is to celebrate Houston's display of its peoples' fully-developed adult ethical intelligence.

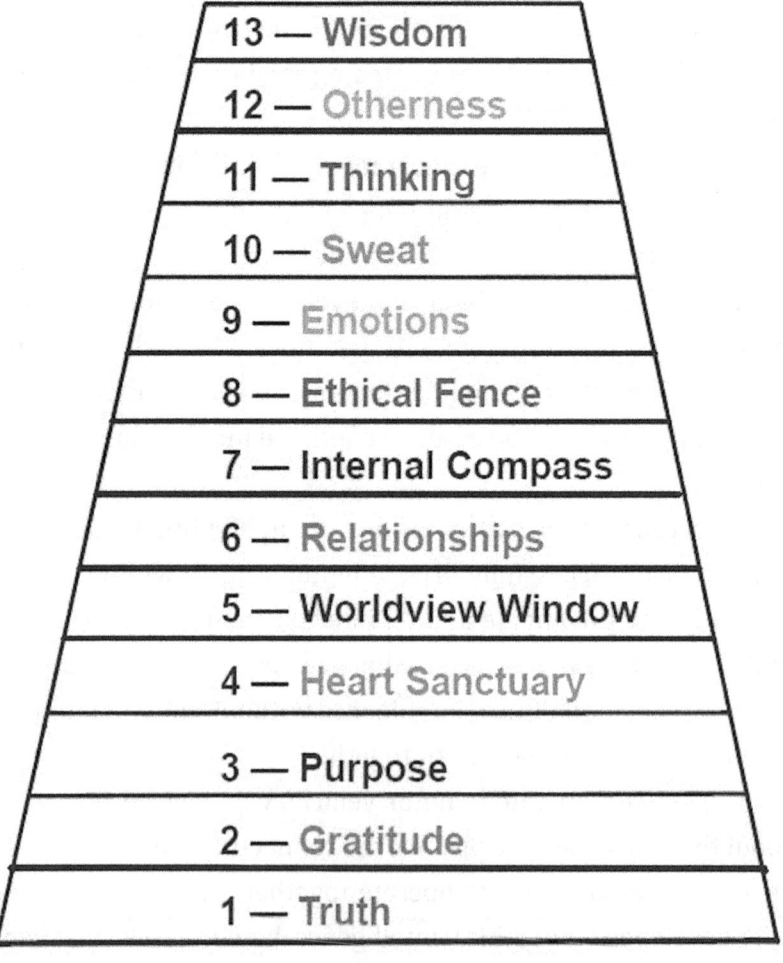

Going Forward. The remaining chapters of this book are loosely organized around the infographic "The Journey from Truth to Wisdom" included nearby and at the back of this book. This infographic is a visual display of my Roadmap to an ethically intelligently life. The journey begins at the foundation level, "Truth", and proceeds through the subsequent levels until reaching the "Wisdom" level.

In this book, we're not following that order. Instead, we're mixing the levels because that mixing enables me to more fully tell the story of Houston's response to hurricane Harvey. Jumping around within levels enhances the storytelling. We'll learn about human ethical intelligence as a byproduct as we focus on the main message.

As we close this chapter, I ask you to recall the opening story in the Introduction to this book where two nameless guys were rescuing people with their boat, as shown in the nearby photo.

For those of us who are still into identity politics, here is some information about those two guys and their passengers. One of the guys was white, the other Asian. The women they rescued were African-American. No! They weren't seeing skin color. They saw other humans in trouble. Our next chapter is about seeing clearly in relationships.

CHAPTER 2

SEEING OTHERS CLEARLY

A Large Truck Rescuing Hurricane Harvey Survivors

The dump truck slowly rumbled through the water. It was an unusually clean dump truck! The truck was bright yellow, sporting a high bed that required a ladder to enter, big chrome side pipes that shot straight into the air, and a driver as colorful as the truck itself. The dump truck could have been entered in next month's monster jam.

Shami, the driver, slipped out of the cab and immediately appeared in the truck bed. He was holding a large bullhorn in his left hand. He was there to rescue people from the rising water and take them to safety. But, he had a few things to say first.

Standing in the bed of that truck, soaked to the skin from the relentless rain, and with his ponytail almost parallel to the ground because of the blowing wind, Shami began his short diatribe.

"I am a Jamaican! And, yes I have three jobs!" Hoping everyone got the joke, Shami continued,

"I came to this country five years ago. I've worked like a slave. I have a home and a family, and this amazing truck, plus two others. I am an immigrant who is a testament to immigrants! And, I hate people who don't like immigrants!

"So, if you don't like immigrants don't bother trying to get into my truck. And, if you voted for Donald Trump in the last election, you are not welcome in my truck! All of you Republicans and other Trump voters can drown for all I care!"

At that point, Shami started loading people into his truck. But, not before asking each one who they voted for in the last election. If they failed his test, he left them standing in the water. Once the truck was full, Shami slid back into the driver seat, turned around and gave everyone still standing in the water the finger, and drove off.

> "And, if you voted for Donald Trump in the last election, you are not welcome in my truck! All of you Republicans and other Trump voters can drown for all I care!"

You're all probably wondering why you didn't see or hear about this story on the news media. You would think our partisan news media would be all over a story like this. Shami would be getting showered with offers to appear on media outlets, regardless of political leanings. Social media would be melting down over his behavior. Shami would be receiving death threats. His family home might even be picketed! A story like this would be hard to miss! So, why haven't we heard about this?

Because this story nor any like it happened! The rain from hurricane Harvey caused a lot of damage and heartache. But, that rain did something else too—it **washed all of our world-**

view windows clean. We saw others clearly. We weren't blinded by skin color, ethnicity, gender, language, sexual orientation, age, height, weight or any other prejudice. We practiced the message of the ancient greeting Namasté—I recognize and acknowledge your humanity. And, because of that, I'll treat you as I would like you to treat me.

Do You See Me?

As I write this book, there is a contemporary television commercial showing a series of different people engaged in various types of activity. Some people are working in an office. Others are playing tennis or changing clothes in a locker room. One person is sitting on a train with tears streaming down her face. And the one question they all ask is, "Do you see me?"

At first hearing, this seems like an odd question. Of course, I can see you. How could I miss you? You're standing or sitting right in front of me. But, **is** that an odd question? How many times have you walked past someone that you knew but didn't acknowledge their presence? Yes, I know! You were looking at your phone! No, that isn't what I'm talking about! That condition is a lapse of mindfulness, a subject for another time.

> We saw others clearly. We weren't blinded by skin color, ethnicity, gender, language, sexual orientation, age, height, weight or any other prejudice.

What the people in the television commercial are talking about is not, "Do you see this collection of molecules in front of you?" No, they're asking, "Are you seeing me as a human being or are you seeing my unsightly skin condition?" The product being advertised is offered as a cure for the often-unsightly skin condition known as psoriasis. I don't know if this commercial is effectively selling this product, but I can tell you, with great confidence, it raises one of the most important issues of our time.

What do we perceive or "know" when we look at or associate with another person, even those with whom we've had a long-term relationship? Here is a story from my personal experience, a story of which I am not particularly proud. And, I consider myself ethically intelligent.

What's In A Name? I've been going to the same hairstylist for more than ten years. Even though I have substantially less hair than I had in my younger days, I am particular about how it looks after a haircut. In fact, even when I was working out of state for a few years, I would wait to have my haircut until I could come home and visit this stylist.

Over the years, I've had many conversations with her, learning the typical things one discovers about a person's family that are the subject of those types of casual conversations. I learned that she and members of her family emigrated from Vietnam many years ago. She arrived in the United States with nothing. But, through hard work and determination, she had built her own thriving business.

Additionally, I had learned she had three children and a husband who worked in the oil business. About a year ago, her husband suddenly died from complications of diabetes. Since her husband's death, her longtime customers tried to help and comfort her. Linda and I both go to her salon, and we've tried to be as helpful as possible.

Several days ago, I went to get my haircut. Of course, the conversation turned to hurricane Harvey, and she began relating her experience. Like our family, the water came near her home, but it didn't flood. Instead, a tornado went through her neighborhood seriously damaging her home. As I listened, I realized she was sharing intimate details of the experience normally reserved for an old friend.

As I continued listening to the details of her storm experience—how terrified she was as she sheltered in a bathtub with her children, how portions of her roof simply disappeared, how the rain poured into her house, how helpless she felt without her husband—my heart was breaking for her. Then, I realize something about this relationship that made me ashamed. **I didn't know her name!**

I've known, no been acquainted with, with this woman for many years. I've admired her success and how that success had translated into her helping her extended family and becoming a model citizen, of the type we say we value. She's important to me, if for no other reason that she expertly cuts my hair and styles it exactly the way I want. **But, I didn't know her name!**

After I had paid for my haircut and was about to leave the salon, I sheepishly asked for her name. You would've thought I had just given her a large check. Her demeanor changed. A big smile brightened her face, she hadn't smiled that way since her husband passed away. She told me her name. I didn't quite understand it. So, I asked her to write it down for me. She proudly wrote "Twee" on the back of one of her salon cards.

Why is something as simple as knowing someone's name so important? There are many reasons. First, it shows you care enough about them to know their name. Second, it validates that person's existence as an equal fellow human. Finally, it adds value to them because acknowledging them by calling out their name adds stature to their place in the universe, and it assures they are not some nameless cog in a grand process.

This incident raised some important personal questions for me. Why didn't I know her name? And, what does it say about me that I didn't know her name, especially after a ten-year relationship. I could offer the excuse that it was just a minor business relationship, one that could have been easily replaced. But, that rationalization doesn't work either.

It doesn't work because, even when I was working and living in another state, I didn't find another hairstylist. I'd wait to return to Houston to get a haircut. That doesn't reflect a minor relationship. No, I had to engage in deeper introspection to make sense of this personal mystery. After a truthful (a subject we'll cover in the next chapter) internal evaluation, I discovered the uncomfortable answer lurking within the engine driving my personal behavior—my ethical intelligence.

My worldview window wasn't nearly as clean as I had imagined. Over time, I'd let it become cloudy and fogged over, the way the inside of my car windshield gets between car washes. I wasn't "seeing" as clearly as I assumed. My focus was fuzzy, kind of like trying to read without wearing my reading glasses. I'd let my internal "housekeeping" slip. Let's examine this idea more closely, why it's important and why Houston passed the "worldview window" test during hurricane Harvey.

Worldview Windows

These days, we don't even have to leave the house to encounter another human being. We "see" them on television, on our computer screens, or on one of our many handheld devices. In fact, we can even have impaired vision and still "see" someone because we visualize the people whose voices we hear. My question is, what is it that we're perceiving? Do we just look right past them, as I apparently was with my hair stylist? Do we perceive them and immediately judge them as unworthy of acknowledgement or irrelevant to our own personal world? If so, why?

About a year ago, I wrote a blog post accompanied by the nearby picture of a homeless man. The blog post later became an article appearing on Facebook, LinkedIn and some other media outlets entitled, "Worthless People." In this article, I asked the question, "Are there any worthless people?" The reaction was fast, overwhelming and surprisingly contentious! I suppose, in today's polarized and politicized world, I shouldn't have been surprised, but I was totally unprepared, shocked and, frankly, troubled at the aftermath.

"What kind of a commie slime ball are you advocating that we should care about someone who is as worthless as this joker?"

In one venue alone, the article garnered more than 600 comments and counter comments. The main point of the article was my belief that no one is worthless. I believe that simply because we're human, we have value. Hence, no one is worthless. I was both praised and excoriated by those commenting on the article.

Here is a brief collection of some of those comments. "How can you be so heartless as to show a picture of a man so down on his luck?" Or, "What kind of a commie slime ball are you advocating that we should care about someone who is as worthless as this joker?" Or, "You're nothing but a liberal wingnut. Spending my tax money helping this piece of crap is a total waste!" Or, "Thank you for showing how unfeeling Republicans are that this man is homeless!" Incidentally, I clean up this language substantially before presenting it here. Oh, and I didn't advocate anything in this article except to say that everyone has value, not equal value just value.

All this commentary was written by people who knew nothing or little about me or my beliefs. Yes, I know! You might say that's incorrect because I have an extensive online presence that anyone can access. But, you'd only be partially correct. I'm careful about what I write and/or say in public places because I don't want to be stereotyped as this or that. There are only two people who know what I truly believe—God and my wife! And neither one of them are talking!

Tribalism, an Original Sin. *How did we get here?* How did we reach a place in our society where we ascribe beliefs and behaviors to people we've neither met nor know anything about? If you haven't asked yourself that question, I urge you to think about it as you read this book. Let's open this discussion with this short story of compassion and bravery starring Todd and Amber, not their real names, of course.

Todd and Amber live in a far Northwest Houston neighborhood. Because they were worried about the potential for flooding at the storage location where they kept their boat, they brought it to their house just prior to the storm and parked the boat on its trailer in their driveway. Todd and Amber's neighborhood had never flooded, even during the tax day flood of 2016. Like most of us, they were unconcerned about any personal flooding danger.

Then, the water rose into the streets in their neighborhood making those streets impassable. The water continued rising, until Todd and Amber had four feet of water in their home, which was just enough water to float the boat from its trailer in their driveway. They knew they had to leave their home. As they were leaving, Todd and Amber started picking up neighbors, taking them to a drop off point where trucks then took those rescued to a local shelter.

During one of the drop-offs, an official told Todd no pets were being accepted at the rescue center. Todd and Amber were instructed not to rescue people with pets because the center would not admit them. We pick up the conversation from there.

Me: "What did you think and say?"

Todd: "Nothing at the time because the wind was blowing at gale force and the rain was torrential. Amber and I just wanted to get people out."

Amber: "I was very angry and hurt that someone would be that cold-hearted. But, I didn't say anything."

Me: "What happened then?"

Todd: "We continued bringing people out. And, then, it happened."

Me: "What happened?"

Amber: "We saw this family of five waving frantically from their roof. My heart sunk."

Me: "Why?"

Todd: "They had two big labs on the roof with them."

Me: "So what did you do?"

Amber: "We went to rescue them."

Me: "And the dogs?"

Todd: "I was going to follow our instructions and rescue only the people. We angled up to the house and tied the boat to the downspout. The people were so relieved."

Helicopter Pet Rescue

Amber: "We explained to them that we couldn't take the dogs. The children broke into tears. It broke my heart, but we had our instructions."

Me: "So, what happened?"

Todd: "I looked at that family and it hit me! That was us so many years ago! Those children looked like our children, and those dogs looked like our dogs back then. It brought tears to my eyes."

Me: "So, what did you do?"

Amber: "We did what we would've wanted them to do for us, if the circumstances were reversed. By God, we rescued them, **including the dogs!**"

Aside from giving us a poignant snapshot of the multiple thousands of acts of goodness displayed during hurricane Harvey, what does this short story tell us? It tells us that we most closely identify with people who look like us, lead lives like ours, hold similar beliefs, and move within similar social economic circles. I know you're probably thinking, *this is not a major revelation*. We all know this! Yes, I agree, but there's something else going on here, under the surface.

CHAPTER 2: SEEING OTHERS CLEARLY

Remember, I asked the question, "How did we get here?" And, "here" refers to our current situation where we ascribe beliefs and characteristics to people we've never met and actually "know" nothing about. This behavior is coming from a strange reversal of the American "melting pot" tradition. We are experiencing a creeping tribalism. Instead of emphasizing our oneness, we're celebrating and elevating our differences, sometimes forcefully.

> We are experiencing a creeping tribalism. Instead of emphasizing our oneness, we're celebrating and elevating our differences, sometimes forcefully.

I've been blessed with a long life, which I'm hoping becomes longer! During that life, I've lived with and among six generations of Americans, starting with my grandparents. My grandparents, on both sides of my family, were immigrants who arrived via Ellis Island. Their desires and dreams for themselves and their children were to become Americans. They had no desire to be known as Polish-Americans or Romanian-Americans.

Their desire was to assimilate into the culture of their new country. Yes, they were proud of their heritage. But, that was secondary to becoming "Americans." And, they were grateful for being in this country. My fraternal grandmother, the only grandparent I knew personally, was proud that her son, my father, contributed to our victory in World War II. But, I also remember the darker side of our culture.

I lived most of my teen years in the 1950s. It was time of great hope and promise. After the end of World War II and the Korean War, the economy was booming. But we lived with black-white segregation, separate but equal schools, separate restrooms, separate water fountains, as shown in the nearby photo from my youth.

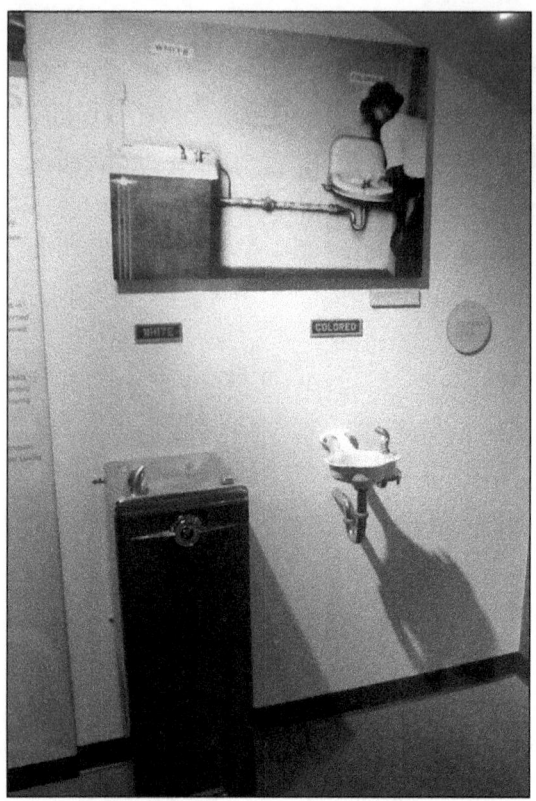
1950s Segregated Fountains

Yes, even in Indiana! In fact, I lived and worked professionally in Detroit in the late 1960s, and the discrimination was far worse than anything I found when I moved to Houston. Family members with continuing relationships in Detroit, tell me little has changed since then. But, that's a subject for another time!

So, the creeping regression to tribalism, separation and segregation I see today is troubling. Trust me, separate but unequal or even equal is not better than togetherness and unity, no matter how difficult its realization. I lived segregation and separation. It isn't pretty and a desirable condition, and we shouldn't be romanticizing its return.

> I lived segregation and separation. It isn't pretty and a desirable condition, and we shouldn't be romanticizing its return.

Worldview and Content of Character. Okay! I'm off my soapbox, for a while anyway! Seriously, what's this got to do with hurricane Harvey and Houston's response? Why is this even important? I'm glad you asked! There's a reason I started this book with the subject. It's not only the root cause of the partisan political polarization in our country but also the gateway to your ethical intelligence. **You can't assess the content of someone's character if you don't "see" them. And, we see others through our worldview window.**

Our worldview window is the prism through which we filter our life experiences. It's a metaphorical window that is saturated by our worldview. And, worldview is our method for extracting meaning from the sensory inputs to our consciousness. Our worldview is initially established by the customs and norms of the culture in which we were raised. Most of us received our early values and opinions from our parents and other family members, including aunts, uncles, and grandparents.

These values and opinions may change over time and become tempered as we mature and grow older, but they remain deeply ingrained within us. I grew up in the Midwest of the United States, my tribe. Although I've traveled the world and lived outside the United States, I still see and interpret the world mostly through a Midwestern Christian tribal worldview. There's nothing intrinsically good or bad about this. It's just the way it is.

I've deliberately used the words tribe and tribal because it's an artifact of our human civilization. And, it's at the root of most of the conflict we see throughout the world and within our own country. Humans became socialized through tribes or societies, which developed worldviews commonly associated with natural, religious or spiritual beliefs. Eventually, these beliefs became biases that clouded the way tribal members saw others who were not of their tribe. **But, not in Houston.**

During hurricane Harvey, few of us saw different "tribes" Here's an example from Sheriff Gonzalez describing a scene from his department's rescue work.

> "My point is, I saw people from different ethnicities, different skin tone, different heights, weights, shapes and sizes. Everybody was extending their hands for help. Us to them. Them to us. Here was the community working with law enforcement. It wasn't, 'we fear police or we're afraid of one another.' It was something I'll always remember. We saw children, seniors, African-Americans and Hispanics. We saw the diversity of our city. It wasn't just one particular race or group of people. We helped everyone. They were so grateful. We were happy helping them! ..."

We need a return to our original motto, *e pluribus unum*—out of many one. We talk about American exceptionalism, and we can argue about what that means. Surely, one of those meanings is we forsake our special-interests and ethnic tribes and join the only one that counts—the human tribe. **Houston is showing the way!**

Diversity is Not Division

We began this chapter with the story of Shami and his dump truck. As it turns out, the story wasn't true. It never happened, much like many of the fake stories that make their way on air and online these days. Fiction is presented as fact. With all its faults, and there are a few like traffic gridlock, Houston is showing the way to a better future. This, almost seven-million-strong-community, demonstrates that diversity does not portend division.

You may be surprised to learn that Houston is the most diverse city in the world! Yes! I know. You want to challenge me on that boast! And, we could engage in a statistical contest because I have mine, you have yours and they have theirs. Here are a few undisputed facts.

We have people from nearly every country in the world living here. There are more than 140 languages spoken in Houston. We have no ethnic majority—37% Hispanic, 37% Anglo, 17% Black and 8% Asian. Houston has over 12,000 restaurants offering more than 70 global cuisines. **Houston is diversity!**

My neighborhood exemplifies this diversity. Our immediate next-door neighbor is a vegetarian Hindu family from India. The father is an engineer. The mother is a well-educated stay-at-home mom, and their oldest daughter just became a medical doctor.

> We have people from nearly every country in the world living here. There are more than 140 languages spoken in Houston.

The family living next door to them is from France. He is an engineer, and she teaches at an international school. The family living next to them enjoys camping. He is a self-employed carpenter-electronic technician who specializes in creating custom home entertainment centers.

My friend, living across our cul-de-sac, is an excellent African-American maxillofacial surgeon whose expertise I have sampled. Finally, the family living next to them is Hispanic, and they race motorcycles. We've all lived together in peace and tranquility since the subdivision was built in 2004, and we all get along just fine!

During hurricane Harvey and its continuing aftermath, Houston has shown the world what ethical intelligence looks like in action. The storm washed our worldview windows clean of bias and prejudice. We demonstrated what happens when we see one another clearly as fellow humans possessing all the rights and privileges that term represents. Now, let's consider the importance of truth.

CHAPTER 3

LIVING IN TRUTH

Rescuers Taking People Out of a Flooded Neighborhood

Jimmy, a Volunteer Civilian Rescuer Tells of His Work.

"We had just pulled the boat out of the water because it was getting dark. We'd been working the neighborhood all day. We were a bit discouraged because even though everyone had water inside their homes, no one wanted to leave." Jimmy continued,

"The water was waist-deep with a strong current. Our process was that we walked alongside the boat, going from house to house following the streets. By dusk, it was getting hard to see, and we were all exhausted. So, we were heading back to the dispatch center."

Jimmy was a civilian volunteer working with a team of other volunteers using one of the team members' private boat, boat trailer and truck. Jimmy and the other team member also brought their personal trucks filled with bottled water, household supplies and other donated items for distribution to survivors.

The team's method of operation was to drive through the flood water to an assigned neighborhood. They would find a high and dry place, park their vehicles and put the boat into the water. As people were rescued, the team would take those rescued to the dry place. Once they had a vehicle-load of survivors, the team would then take those rescued to a designated shelter. Jimmy picked up the story,

"Just as we were loaded up and headed back to the central command, dispatch called us and said a family in the subdivision that we had been searching all day had called for a rescue. One of the family members had become ill, and a helicopter had been dispatched to pick him up and take him to a medical facility. Our situation had just become a nightmare scenario."

> "This was scary work! Walking in this snake infested water during the day was hard, walking in it when you can't see anything is almost beyond description."

"It was now completely dark, the power was out, so we had no lights, except for flashlights and the lights on our phones. We unloaded the boat from the trailer, and we launched into the water and headed back into the subdivision. This was scary work! Walking in this snake infested water during the day was hard, walking in it when you can't see anything is almost beyond description.

"Using the GPS on our phones, we worked our way back

into the subdivision and found the appropriate house. We loaded the family into the boat and headed back to our trucks. Got everything loaded up, including all the people. And got ready to head to our designated rescue center.

"Just as we were about to get on the road, the mother asked where we were taking them. We told her we were taking them to the nearest accessible rescue center." The mother got out of the truck and started screaming,

"'NO, NO, NO, you have to take us to the medical center where they took my son!'"

Helicopter Flood Rescue

Even though I was interviewing Jimmy the week after this episode had occurred, the irritation and frustration was still palpable in his voice. I could easily understand his response. First, the team had already patrolled this neighborhood during daylight, and everyone had refused to leave, including this family. Second, risking their own personal safety by executing a water rescue in the dark, the team had nonetheless rescued the family. Then, to top it all off, this mother was objecting to the rescue destination!

Her concerns were understandable but not addressable. Jimmy continued with his story,

"The mother was hysterical. So, in their infinite wisdom, the team elected me to talk to her. I got out of my truck and went to speak to her. She kept screaming to me on how she had to be with her sick son. I let her vent for a few moments. Then, after she quit screaming, I looked her in the eyes and said,

"You have a decision to make. You can either come with us to the designated rescue center, or you can stay here in the dark and wait in this rising water until we can dispatch another helicopter to take you to the medical center. Our trucks can't get to the medical center because of the flooding. So, it's your decision!

"I got back into my truck. We waited for a few minutes, and the mother climbed back into the truck. We dropped them off at the rescue center."

Jimmy had just described a moment of truth.

Moments of Truth

The distraught and rescued mother, that Jimmy encountered, was forced to face an unavoidable and clearly unmistakable moment of truth. Options that she imagined and hoped were available, were not. Choices she believed were her right to make, she could not. She was faced with two unwanted and unpleasant choices— remain at her present location standing in the dangerous floodwater she was desperately trying to escape, or go to a location that didn't include her sick son.

As I interviewed people, I asked them a series of standard questions. One of those questions was, "When did you know it was time to leave your home?" I asked this question because answering it reveals a moment of truth to the person providing the answer. Please note, even though I show these as direct quotes, I had to paraphrase and make some of the answers family-friendly. I'll go first and provide my response to the question— **"When did you know it was time to leave your home?"**

CHAPTER 3: LIVING IN TRUTH

Author's Street

Me: "I realized it was time to leave when I couldn't. My situation was reinforced when I saw the National Guard truck shown in the nearby photo rescuing some neighbors on my street."

Fred: "We were afraid to leave because we didn't have insurance, and we weren't sure our stuff would be there when we got back. We left when everything in our house was ruined by the water anyway."

Thomas: "We left when the water rose two feet in less than 30 minutes. At that rate, I could tell I had to get my family out of there. By the time the boat came to get us, the water in the living room was up to my waist!"

Mia: "We stayed too long. We thought we could wait it out upstairs. But, then, we realized the danger of being in a house surrounded by over ten feet of water!"

Lakeisha: "When we ran out of food for my babies. I didn't think we would be stranded for more than a day, maybe two."

Manny: "When the power went out."

Bob: "When I swung my feet over the side of my bed and they landed in six inches of water! That was quite a shock."

Amber: "When the water got so high, it floated the boat right off the trailer parked in our driveway!"

Don: "I was determined to stay, no matter what. We left when I could see the fear in my wife's eyes."

Gwen: "When the boats came down the street, and my neighbors were leaving. The thought of being left alone in all that water was too much!"

Now, that we've experienced a few moments of truth, let's make the point behind the questions. Frequently, we lie to ourselves. For any number of reasons, we refuse to acknowledge what our senses are presenting to our consciousness. Sometimes, this is unavoidable because our brains present us with faulty information. Or, we're suffering from some type of trauma. Or, we've prejudged someone or something.

The point is that we often disregard the most logical conclusion from a set of facts, as best as we know those facts, because the logical conclusion makes us uncomfortable. Or, it challenges our worldview and calls into question some of our beliefs. Or, the logical conclusion is too frightening to confront. Or, ... fill in the blank. The point is we lie to ourselves, sometimes at great peril.

Here's Marie's story, as related to me by one of my students.

"Mom moved in with us three years ago. We had an unused room over the garage that we turned it into a small apartment for her. It worked out well because it had a separate entrance, and she could come and go anytime she wanted.

"We weren't too concerned about hurricane Harvey because our house and location had been high and dry ever since we lived here. Then, came that Sunday when the water started rising in the street. Within a couple of hours, it was already up our driveway.

"I told Tom I thought we ought to bring mom into the house just in case the water kept rising. He was glued to the television watching the weather reports. He was insisting that in the 22 years we lived here the water had never risen high enough to get into the house. So, we waited.

"As it turned out, mom wasn't any more interested in coming into the house than Tom was in bringing her in. We kept texting back and forth, and she said that she would be just fine in her apartment. The rain continued pouring. So, we went upstairs to our game room to watch the television.

"Just as it started getting dark, the power went out. I got a frantic text from my mom. She said she had tried to leave her apartment, and she couldn't. Water had come up fast, and it was up to her waist. I frantically headed down the stairs and was shocked to find three feet of water on first floor.

"I yelled for Tom. Then, I heard loud voices out on the

driveway. I waded out the back door and found my mom half way of the stairs to her apartment arguing with three guys holding a rubber boat. They wanted her to get into the boat so they could rescue her. She was resisting. Normally, I would've been suspicious of three guys covered in tattoos standing in my driveway at dusk, too. But, this was anything but normal.

"I calmed her down and helped mom get into the boat. She leaned over and whispered into my ear, 'These guys look like gang members. Why are we trusting them?' I gave her that "daughter/mother" look that says it's okay. About that time, my stubborn husband came out the backdoor with a plastic bag full of stuff.

"We got into the boat, and these three guys took us out of the neighborhood. The rain was pouring, and the wind was blowing. None of us said anything. We were all too embarrassed at how we acted. We thanked the three guys, and they went back into the neighborhood."

I asked my student if she could arrange an interview with Marie. After several weeks, I learned that Marie had no further interest in talking about the incident. The fact that Marie was too embarrassed to talk to me about this story, says much positive about her character. I would also be embarrassed. What else does the story teach us about truth?

> We often evaluate the "facts" of the situation and come to the wrong conclusion because the correct conclusion is too difficult to accept.

There are two lies in this story. First, Tom lied to himself about the gravity of the situation. I can identify with Tom because my house had never flooded before, either. We often evalu-

National Guard Rescue Trucks in My (Author's) Neighborhood.

ate the "facts" of the situation and come to the wrong conclusion because the correct conclusion is too difficult to accept. Or, we simply don't believe the "facts" our lyin' eyes are telling us.

The second lie in this case is prejudice. Again, I can identify with this circumstance. Although I live in a safe neighborhood, we see people carjacked and robbed in their driveway on the local news almost every night. So, fear of three unknown guys appearing in your driveway at dusk is not unreasonable, especially if your worldview window reveals them as "gang members."

Here are some examples. Oh, "The drug paraphernalia I found in my child's bedroom must belong to someone else". Or, "This persistent bruise I've had on my leg for the last six months is just an old football injury". Or, "The rain forecasts for hurricane Harvey must be wrong because these weather forecasters never get it right". Or, "Even if these forecasts are correct, my neighborhood has never flooded. So, I don't need to be concerned, until I see the National Guard rescue trucks shown in a nearby picture".

You might be asking, "So, what's the big deal? This is just part of life. It's rationalization." The big deal is truth and telling the truth all the time is the foundation of ethical intelligence. We start our truth-telling by telling ourselves the truth all the time. And, we demand others tell us the truth.

Aha! But, there's a potential problem here, isn't there? Not all of us agree on the definition of truth. The meaning of truth to me may be different from your meaning. Your "facts" may not mean the same as mine. These objections recall that certain Roman Governor's ancient question, "What is truth?"

What is Truth?

If you pay attention to the cultural discourse taking place in our society, no one would blame you if you concluded there is no such thing as truth. Today, we hear a lot about "fake" news. A recent survey from a reputable research group concluded that over 70% of published news stories are either false or based on questionable "facts." So, what are we mere mortals to do?

The answer to that question is do your own research. Find out, as best you can what the "facts" are. But, that doesn't answer the question of what truth is. Incidentally, I'm not talking about ultimate truth. I'll leave that discussion to philosophers, scientists and theologians. No, what we're talking about here is a congruence between what you believe about a circumstance and what you report.

Based on that premise, my working definition of truth is, truthfulness is telling or having the intention of telling the truth, which is defined as accurately and sincerely describing reality (including the context of that reality), as known by the person describing that reality.

So, if you see a creature that looks like something you've been taught is a duck and you report that you've seen a duck, you're telling the truth. If we later find out that what you saw was not a duck but something else, you're not a liar. You reported what you thought was a duck. But, you were wrong. Incidentally, this is why eyewitness testimony is so unreliable, especially during emergencies.

Why is this important? Because, too many of us believe, rightly or wrongly, that public officials don't tell the truth. That belief may be generally correct, but I don't think it was true during the response to hurricane Harvey. Here's why.

For several days prior to the hurricane Harvey's landfall, weather forecasters continuously warned us about catastrophic flooding. Because we'd never experienced that level of flooding, most of us didn't take those warnings as seriously as we should have. Additionally, during the nine years since hurricane Ike ravaged the Houston area in 2008, more than one million people had moved to the Houston area. Those new residents would've certainly had no idea of the magnitude of potential flooding.

When the torrential rains came and suddenly filled the drainage systems to capacity and began overflowing, water poured into both business and residential areas at a ferocious pace. In some cases, water was rising at the rate of two or more feet per hour. Many were caught completely off guard with several inches of water in their homes, business or parking lot with no warning, as shown in the nearby photo. Panic, fear and anger ensued.

Being caught off guard with little to no warning was a common theme in my discussions with survivors. It's one circumstance to see floodwaters slowly encroaching your location but quite another to suddenly find yourself standing in water inside your home or business. In the first case, you can assemble important documents and other artifacts for safekeeping. In the latter case, you're forced to flee to save your life.

Our local news media did an excellent job documenting the unfolding disaster. We saw pictures of water lapping at rooftops, people being rescued by helicopter and cries for help from people on local talk radio. Social media also painted a dire picture of our circumstances. Many people were posting cries for help on social media. Our collective psyche was inundated with the seemingly escalating perils of the disaster.

On live television, we saw a local television studio overrun by flood waters. The newsroom staff had to quickly relocate to higher ground. We witnessed the heroics of a local TV reporter saving the life of a drowning truck driver. Even in locations where flooding was minimal, the air seemed filled with looming tragedy. Ordinary people felt compelled to do something.

Those conditions crowdsourced an army of civilian volunteer rescuers, using whatever they had at hand to enter the battle. I started this chapter with Jimmy's story. He was one of those civilian volunteer rescuers. I asked him what it was like as they did their work. He began with a one-word answer,

Jimmy: "Chaos! We were all rushing around trying to help, but communication was difficult."

Me: "How did you get started?"

Jimmy: "Social media. Three guys who owned an auto service company organized a group. And, I joined with them. They moved the central location three times because the group just kept getting bigger and bigger."

Me: "How did you get organized."

Jimmy: "We were assigned to teams and a boat and got started."

Me: "How did you know where to go?"

Jimmy: "There was a central dispatch that told us where to go for rescues."

Me: "Who organized central dispatch?"

Jimmy: "I am not sure. It changed several times. And, this was one of the biggest problems."

Me: "What do you mean?"

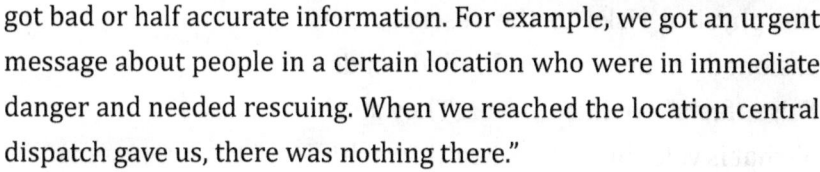

Jimmy: "We continually got bad or half accurate information. For example, we got an urgent message about people in a certain location who were in immediate danger and needed rescuing. When we reached the location central dispatch gave us, there was nothing there."

Me: "Nothing there?"

Jimmy: "Yes, the location didn't exist. We wasted more than an hour driving on nearly impassable flooded roads only to find nothing!"

Me: "How often did this happen?"

Jimmy: "A lot. It was one of the most frustrating problems we had. Good information was hard to come by."

What do you conclude from this story? Was Jimmy's team receiving lies? Were they receiving misinformation? Could they have been receiving the truth? What is true here? As you can see, answering these questions is a bit complicated. Why does it matter, anyway?

Truth and Consequences

Truth or its absence has consequences. We see that in the previous story. Operating under a set of "facts", Jimmy's team not only didn't achieve their purpose—rescuing people in distress—but also wasted precious resources when those resources were sorely needed. There are questions about the "misinformation" perpetrated during those rescue efforts. We're not going to try and answer those questions because that's not our mission. The important point for us to internalize is **truth or its absence has consequences.**

What are those consequences? In this case, it was lost time, a lost opportunity to rescue someone else and wear and tear on the vehicles and other assets in use. And, this doesn't include the physical risks to the rescuers occasioned by driving on flooded roads. False "facts" are like thieves. They steal all that is valuable to us—health, wealth and relationships. And, most importantly, false "facts", whether provided intentionally or not, steal our freedom.

Society crumbles when most information in the public sphere is misleading, lacking context or simply false. A civilized society is built on a foundation of law and standards of public behavior. A free society lives on trust. We trust public officials, including law enforcement, to act in our best interests because they take an oath proclaiming "public" service. We trust that public officials' pronouncements are true. Believing otherwise is corrosive to the society. Here's a recent and instructive example from outside Houston.

Early in October, 2017, a mass murder occurred during a country music festival in Las Vegas Nevada. Over the weeks after the event, the "facts" of the tragedy "evolved" or changed completely—more than once. First, there was a lone shooter with no accomplices. Then, there were multiple shooters with several accomplices. Finally, as I write this book, we have a lone shooter with a possible accomplice.

In the beginning of the investigation, a hotel security guard was shot in the leg **after** the lone shooter had finished killing the victims. Later, we learned the security guard was shot in the leg **before** the shooter began shooting. Then, the security guard mysteriously disappeared with no one aware of his whereabouts. Suddenly, the security guard reappeared on a television talk show, exhibiting deceitful body language.

Then, we learned that the FBI confiscated all the cell phones of the massacre audience members. Sometime later, the cell phones were returned to the owners completely wiped clean of any information, including the owners' personal information unrelated to the massacre. To date, there's been no public or private explanation of this behavior.

The Clark County Sheriff recently announced that he was dispensing with periodic briefings about the investigation. The FBI has held few briefings and dispensed little information about the investigation. The official "facts" about the incident and the subsequent investigation have often been contradictory and seemingly implausible.

Citizen and professional journalists have poured into this information void trying to uncover the "facts." Much of this effort has produced information that is different from the official pronouncements. Criminal justice and law enforcement officials uninvolved in the investigation appear on television and various

Houston Mayor Turner and Texas Governor Abbot.

radio programs analyzing what they believe happened. The result has been a wide public perception that these public officials are neither competent nor truthful.

Their combined credibility has steadily declined since the event occurred. And, there has been a steady erosion of the public's trust in these public officials. Finally, and worse, numerous conspiracy theories have arisen due to the dearth of believable information. This incident, in which 58 people died and more than 500 were wounded, seems destined to become another JFK assassination "grassy-knoll" conspiracy.

Truth is the foundation of a fully-developed adult ethical intelligence. **Houston's response to the aftermath of hurricane Harvey showed that truth can prevail.** Jimmy's incorrect information was a product of chaos. No one was deliberately attempting to deceive.

Unlike Las Vegas, during hurricane Harvey, **our public officials spoke the truth** as well as the circumstances allowed. For that, we should thank them, shown in a nearby photo, because it's helped us squarely face our circumstances, plan for recovery and rebuild our great city.

Next, we consider serving in silence—the model for living a life of gratitude within healthy and fulfilling relationships.

CHAPTER 4

SERVING IN SILENCE

Samaritan's Purse Volunteers Helping Hurricane Harvey Survivors

Ron, a Compassionate Metro Driver. The Metro Special Services van rounded the corner and headed down the once-idyllic-tree-lined street in a modest older Northeast Houston neighborhood. Both sides of the street were piled high with construction debris pulled out of flooded homes. The van driver, Ron a retired Army sergeant, casually observed that the debris was falling into the drainage ditches on both sides of the street, potentially blocking runoff from the next rain.

Finally, the van came to a stop in front of a small nondescript two-bedroom home built on a cramped lot, surrounded by a four-foot high chain-link fence. The house badly needed new paint, and

the yard hadn't been mowed in such a long time, seed pods were beginning to open. A rusted old wheelbarrow and a junk push lawnmower hinted at the emerging frailties of the returning residents.

It was a trademark hot and steamy early September day in Houston. The dripping air was deadly still and carried the stench of mold and mildew. The artifacts of the recent flooding were easily visible—water marks on structures, silt in the street, trash and litter everywhere and that nasty smell of rotting materials, including long-spoiled food.

Snakes, forced into the open by the flood waters, slithered nearby, eager to feast on the copious collection of rats and other rodents attracted to the spoiled and putrid food. An occasional crowing rooster pierced the morning air, a testament to the unique nature of this long-neglected and forgotten heavily-wooded neighborhood (depicted in a nearby photo) situated amidst the fourth largest city in the country.

Ron jumped out of the vehicle and into the sauna-like conditions, cursing the Houston weather. He lowered the wheelchair to the street and helped Pete Miller, a retired construction worker its owner, into the chair. He wheeled Pete and the wheelchair up the dirt path to the old-timey porch on the front of the house and returned to the van to help Marie, Pete's wife make the same journey up the path. After escorting Marie up to the porch, Ron asked if they needed any assistance getting inside.

CHAPTER 4: SERVING IN SILENCE

This was the Miller's first time back to their home since being rescued by boat during the surprise-flooding of their neighborhood. Their neighborhood had never flooded before, and they were caught off guard with the almost instantaneous appearance of two feet of water in their home. A rescue boat brought them out just before another two feet of water rushed into the neighborhood.

Pete and Marie had left so quickly they were unable to take any of their possessions with them. Now, faced with opening the door to the house, they both feared the worst. Ron opened the rickety front door, and the small amount of water remaining in the house flowed out carrying with it a few small snakes, dead rodents and water-soaked papers and pictures.

> Marie gasped, almost collapsing to the ground sobbing uncontrollably. After 52 years of marriage and no children, this small house was all they had left.

Marie gasped, almost collapsing to the ground sobbing uncontrollably. After 52 years of marriage and no children, this small house was all they had left. Ron ventured inside the structure, opened some windows and quickly returned, gasping for air. The air inside the house was so toxic it brought tears to his eyes. The window air conditioner was inoperable making the interior of the home at least 20° hotter than the outside air. He asked the couple if they wanted to stay or return to the rescue center.

Through clenched teeth, mustering a faltering voice and with small tears trickling down his cheeks, Pete defiantly said, "No, we're stayin'!" Ron noticed Marie nodding in agreement. Marie told him that they would make some calls to friends and neighbors to see if someone could help. Reluctantly, Ron left Pete and Marie on the porch of their wrecked home and continued his Metro route. As he drove, the thought of this elderly couple sitting in the sweltering Houston heat continued gnawing at Ron. Finally, after dropping off his last passenger, Ron called his church and explained Pete and Marie's situation to one of the associate pastors. The church's Harvey volunteer group sprang into action.

Within hours, the church had dispatched a team of volunteers who also hand-delivered a $1,000 check to Pete and Marie. Over the subsequent weeks, the team of volunteers completely rebuilt the house, including exterior painting, air conditioning replacement and landscaping. They even sold the old push lawnmower to a collector!

> ... the team of volunteers completely rebuilt the house, including exterior painting, air conditioning replacement and landscaping.

Gratitude, Currency of the Universe

Pete and Marie were overwhelmed with the unsolicited and unexpected outpouring of respect, kindness and charity from complete strangers. Gratitude filled their modest home like a sweet shared fragrance. Yes, there was volunteer gratitude! Gratitude for the opportunity to serve others just like themselves. Many of the volunteers also had been wiped out by the flood waters, and others had helped them. **Gratitude is the currency of the universe.** So, what exactly is gratitude?

Gratitude. Gratitude is an emotion expressing appreciation for what you have. The dictionary defines gratitude as the quality of being thankful, including a readiness to show appreciation for and to return kindness. Often, we show gratitude with a hug, as in the nearby Harvey survivor photo.

Gratitude has long been an emotion associated with religious practice, and all the world's religions encourage gratitude as an essential element of moral practice. Since antiquity, philosophers have studied, theorized and recommended the virtue of gratitude. Gratitude has also been associated with spirituality. And, during the past decade, psychologists and others have begun studying gratitude.

Those studies have shown that grateful people are happier, less depressed, less stressed and more satisfied with their lives and relationships. So, if you want to experience more positive emotions, feel more deeply alive, sleep better and even strengthen your immune system, be intentionally grateful for even the smallest things that you have. Neuroscientists have demonstrated that intentional gratitude rewires our brains in positive ways. As you might imagine, in our gadget-centric world, there are even apps for this purpose.

> Our human nature is not hardwired for gratitude. In my experience, it's just the opposite. For every grateful and happy person we meet, we encounter five complainers.

Our human nature is not hardwired for gratitude. In my experience, it's just the opposite. For every grateful and happy person we meet, we encounter five complainers. I once worked for a CEO whose approach to life was to look for what was wrong rather than what was right in every situation. He was an unhappy man and those who worked for him became unhappy and complainers. The result, except for his admin, he didn't have any long-term staff members.

So why is gratitude a key to living an ethically intelligent life? Being grateful requires humility and mindfulness. It requires us to respect insignificance. When we're grateful for the small things in life, gratefulness opens our minds and spirit so that we can "see" the people in our lives the world considers insignificant. Gratitude helps us maintain an open and clear Worldview Window.

Cathy Pam, appearing in the nearby iconic photo, expressed gratitude for being rescued by Daryl Hudeck of the Houston SWAT Team. We're grateful for the use of this picture, which appeared in hundreds of publications and was seen by millions of people from around the word.

I am a poster child for the reality that we're not naturally grateful. Being grateful is a recent behavioral change for me. I once took all I had for granted, almost to the point of seeing my gifts as entitlements. When one of those gifts disappears, you become keenly aware not only of its loss, but it's importance. How many times have you heard someone say "I wish I would've told her how important she was?" Or, "I always meant to thank him for how well he did his job." Don't wait. Begin today.

Gratitude is a learned behavior. Using whatever works for you, I encourage you to intentionally express gratitude for something at least twice a day. Maintain a log or journal. Record your gratefulness. Intentionality is important. Significance is not. You don't have to wait for that "big" event to express gratitude. Be grateful that you have a place to live and clean water to drink, many in the world don't. Or, next time the elevator is out of order, be thankful that you can climb the stairs.

Cicero said, "Gratitude is not only the greatest of virtues, but the parent of all the others." I hope you now see, gratitude is as contagious as the common cold—except gratitude is good for you. Gratitude fills your heart with love. It exchanges mourning for joy. It's like a healing balm soothing a troubled spirit. Gratitude covers a multitude of ailments. It dissolves a cynical attitude and encourages hope. Gratitude is an essential element of a fully-developed human ethical intelligence. Don't neglect it.

> "What would you have tomorrow if your tomorrow contained only that for which you'd expressed gratitude the day before?"

A wise person once posed this question, "What would you have tomorrow if your tomorrow contained only that for which you'd expressed gratitude the day before?" I encourage you to ask yourself that question every morning as you prepare for the day. You might be surprised at the barrenness of your world, absent expressions of gratitude during the prior day. Don't neglect expressions of gratitude. It's good for you and those around you!

Okay! I see the rolling eyes. I hear the muffled murmurs. No, I don't live your life. I don't know how bad your job is. And, I don't know how badly your kids get on your nerves! What I do know

is you have to breathe just like me. Taking a deep breath of fresh clean air is not possible in many places. Just ask the people who live in Beijing, China, shown in the nearby picture. Or, talk to someone with COPD. For many with compromised lungs, taking a deep breath is a distant memory. What? Have I driven in *Houston* traffic?

Yes, I know all about Houston traffic. But, I think you need a functioning car to experience that traffic, right? You also need the income stream necessary to pay the insurance premiums and buy fuel, right? Oh, I see. You don't have time for saying thank you or being intentionally grateful. Well, next time you're sitting in traffic with nothing else to do but fret about being late for your next meeting, try being thankful. Here's an example of how easy this is.

First thing every morning I spend time in prayer and meditation. Here's a small part of my declarations from this morning. "Thank you for this clean air that fills my strong voluminous lungs. Thank you for my powerful heart that supplies my body with nutrients and oxygen. Thank you for the coffee I'm drinking and the home in which I'm standing. Thank you for the clothes I wear, the car I drive, and these two precious creatures laying at my feet...." I think you get the picture. Being thankful and expressing gratitude takes less time than brushing your teeth. Don't neglect expressions of gratitude. It's good for you!

Incidentally, Pete and Marie's experience was not just a one-time event, either. Ron's church alone fielded more than 2,500 volunteers who continued serving in silence months after the cameras went dark and the microphones muted. Hundreds of other organizations performed similar acts of unexpected kindness and goodness.

Although out of sight and out of mind, the goodness continues!

Unsung Heroes, Unexpected Relationships

The cameras are now gone. News crews have long departed, moving on to other disasters and news stories. hurricane Irma blazed a path through Florida. Mexico experienced a major earthquake.  Hurricane Maria practically destroyed the island of Puerto Rico. Hurricane Harvey and Houston are now but a faint moment in the national memory, except for, perhaps, the triumphal victory of the Houston Astros in the 2017 World Series. But, the suffering lingers still, as shown in a nearby photo of Harvey survivors waiting in line for food benefits in mid-October.

And, so did the goodness! It had to. As I write this chapter, we still have more than 24,000 hurricane Harvey survivors living in hotels or other temporary housing. There are countless thousands of families still displaced from their homes. FEMA, the SBA and other governmental agencies are stretched thin dealing with three major disasters. Thousands of businesses are still rebuilding, and the multiple-thousands of people who worked for those businesses are still without paychecks.

Construction materials and workers are in short supply. The housing market has been turned upside down. Quick-buck artists have descended upon Houston offering survivors fifty cents on the dollar for their damaged homes, with many accepting. Charities have received multimillions of dollars of donations and are absent the staff and infrastructure for effectively using the funds. Yet, through it all, there is a palpable spirit of hope and promise. People are receiving help. Volunteers continue serving in silence. The goodness continues. Here's a further example of unsung heroes and gratitude all wrapped together, as related to me by Chief Art Acevedo.

> 'There was a little bit of a debate. Other agencies said this Cajun Navy and these other volunteers have come in with their boats and equipment. Another agency reaction was well they're not trained and this and that. My mindset was: 1) People that need rescue don't care if it's a person that's in a police uniform, a fire uniform or some crazy Cajun. 2) These people, this Cajun Navy, from my perspective, they operate those airboats out there in the swamps.
>
> "They kill alligators with their bare hands! I'd rather be with those folks who know how to survive rescuing me than the so-called trained professionals. We were very proud of

those volunteers. So many other agencies didn't want to use them. But my perspective was that if my family needed rescuing I'll take any boat that comes. Police chief Art Acevedo appears in the nearby photo."

Contrary to other public officials, Chief Acevedo gladly enlisted the civilian volunteers into the cause of saving lives. He was grateful for their help. His visceral reaction to lives in danger led him to decide that, in the case of life and death, any rescue was preferable to no rescue. He outlined his plan.

"They kill alligators with their bare hands! I'd rather be with those folks who know how to survive rescuing me than the so-called trained professionals. We were very proud of those volunteers."

"So, I came back to headquarters one day, and I decided we've gotta be action oriented. We can't be process oriented. We've got to be results oriented. We've got to concentrate on outcomes. I came back and went to the 10th floor of the HPD headquarters and told everyone this department's going rogue. We're officially going rogue, right now.

Houston Police Chief Art Acevedo

"I want us to identify eight staging areas for all these people with boats and equipment that are coming in to volunteer. I want a Lieutenant, and I want a Sergeant assigned to each of these staging areas. We're putting these people and their boats to work. And our cops started working with these folks. Our cops were out in the water at night with them using *flashlights. They were in the water with flashlights as the only lighting. We couldn't get floodlights.*

"And so, once we created those staging areas, we tweeted the information out. We put everybody to work. And it really, really had a big impact. So, at our last count, the police department and volunteer teams rescued over 6,000 people. We eventually stopped counting because we were so damned busy. That's huge! Because we had everyone on 24-hour shifts nobody left. I'm very proud of that.

"More than 550 of our people had their personal homes flooded and not one of them left duty. Our officers stayed working, even knowing that their own families were being rescued. Knowing that their own children were being evacuated out of second story windows because their homes were already flooded.

"There was a lot of heroism! Hopefully, one day, all those stories will be told. I'm very proud of our folks and the citizen volunteers. There was a lot of actual heroism both from law enforcement and from the community itself. I am so grateful for the response we got both from our folks and the volunteers."

Houston Police Chief, Art Acevedo, was answering my question about his department's response to the thousands of civilian volunteers. I agree with his assessment! I've talked to many of those folks who not only used their own resources but also put their safety and lives on the line to help their neighbors, many they had never met and would never see again. Those volunteers were truly heroes and great citizens!

Hurricane Harvey reified thousands of existing relationships. Harvey also created millions of unexpected relationships. Here's example of each from Don and Nancy.

CHAPTER 4: SERVING IN SILENCE

Don: *"The storm made landfall at Rockport on Friday evening. We were keenly watching the weather forecasts because of the potential for heavy rainfall. It rained all day Saturday off and on. We went to bed early Saturday evening knowing that it was going to rain hard all-night long. I tossed and turned for several hours listening to the rain pounding the roof. "I got up early in the morning and turned the television set on. I was watching as the hurricane made its way and then stopped. It continued to rain heavily. I looked out the front window of the house, and I couldn't see much because it was still dark.*

I turned on the television, and I sat watching the weather radar as rain bands continued flowing in from the Gulf.

High-Water Rescue

"I sat transfixed by the radar, periodically getting up to look out the window to see if I could see any rising water in front of our house. I couldn't. So, I continued watching the weather coverage." Nancy came into the living room and said,

Nancy: *"What's going on?"* Don replied,

Don: *"I said I been watching the coverage, and if you look out our front door, you can see the water is rising quickly. Dawn broke, and I could clearly see the water rising in our street. Within hours, the water had risen up to the door and started coming in the front part of the house.*

"Within a short time the water was up to our front windows and was pouring into the house. I knew I had to find a way to get out. I called Carl, a friend of mine who was sever-

al miles away and not having any flooding issues. I told Carl I had to get out of the house. He said he would find a way to get to me with his truck.

"Before I realized, the water inside the house was up to our waist. I had to figure out a way to get my two young children and my wife to safety. About that time, we heard a knock on the door. I went and opened the door and found two men with a small boat. I don't know where they come from, but they asked us if we needed a way out of the neighborhood.

"We grabbed what we could and put the kids in the boat. We walked out of the neighborhood next to the boat in chest-deep water. We finally got to high ground. And, then, into a makeshift rescue center. Later that day Carl came to the rescue center and took us to his house."

Neighbors Rescuing Neighbors

You may be wondering why I've dropped this story here. It seems so like others I've already related. Yes, thankfully it is similar! Since Harvey made landfall, multiple thousands of stories like this have played out as people willingly helped one another, many with the same needs as those they helped. The significance of placing this story here is it demonstrates the importance of relationships. Remember, we can only see the fruits of our ethical intelligence within our relationships.

In addition to the relationship Don has with Nancy, we have two other relationships in the story. The first, is the formation of an unexpected relationship with the two strangers offering the small boat. The second relationship is the continuing friendship of Don and Carl. Clearly, Don had expectations of his relationship with Carl. Don didn't and couldn't have expectations of the two strangers with the small boat. There is, however, a common denominator—gratitude. Gratitude is present and necessary in both relationships.

GRATITUDE OPENS AND SUSTAINS RELATIONSHIPS

Relationships are like soil. Ethical intelligence lives within your consciousness, but it shows up in the real world within a relationship, which is its soil, garden or field. In the following story from Sheriff Gonzalez, water was the "soil", a kind of hydroponic garden.

Deputy Sheriff Rescuing Children

> "We were out around the CE King Parkway, Lake Houston Parkway and the Beltway. We were in that neighborhood rescuing people. They were climbing down off a high-riding-5-ton vehicle that we were using for water rescues. My officers were helping them climb out of the vehicle one at a time, carrying their belongings. It was like a scene out of a disaster movie. The people were like war refugees carrying plastic bags full of whatever they could salvage. They had their pets and small children. They were grateful we were there to help.

As the Sheriff told me this story, the humble pride he felt for our city and its people was palpable. He and his deputies, one of whom is shown rescuing two children in the nearby photo, were grateful for the opportunity to help so many. Sheriff Gonzalez continued his reflection.

> "Later that week, I was talking to some of the national media at the convention center. We were doing a walkthrough, and I asked them, 'What have been your impressions?' Their comments were, 'Oh, this is so unique, it's the way you people work together. You have resources here for the children, medical supplies and everything. It's like you all really take care of one another. You know we don't always see this. In many places the attitude is, 'Well, we got you out. That's it. Houston is different. It's a unique place.'"

Here is another hydroponic relationship garden, as described by a volunteer civilian rescuer. This set of relationships was a bit more challenging.

> "It was the second day, I think. We were out rescuin' people. Most of our boat crew was ex-military. We had a couple of guys who had seen combat, one in Iraqi and the other in Afghanistan. We were doin' so many rescues, my days and the details are kinda hazy. But it was late afternoon when we got the call.
> "The neighborhood, I think it was on the northeast side of town. It was seein' fast rising water, and there were lots of people calling for rescues. There was high water everywhere. So, it took us quite a while to reach the neighborhood and find a staging point to park the truck and boat trailer. It was star-

tin' to get dark, and the rain was coming down again.

"So, we headed into the neighborhood. As we had done before, two guys walked alongside the boat. The water was about waist deep. We got to the first address dispatch had given us, and we got an elderly woman with her son into the boat. We started out for the second address. This neighborhood had a lot of big trees, that and the fact that it was dusk, made it hard to see.

"We got to the second address and we headed up towards the house. Suddenly, we heard what sounded like firecrackers going off. Bill, who was steering the boat said, 'Who in the hell would be fullin' around with firecrackers at a time like this?' Mark, one of our ex-military guys said, 'Shit, those sounds you're hearin' aren't firecrackers, they're gunshots.

"We heard some more, BANG, BANG, BANG! One of the bullets tore through the side of the boat. Jim, who was wading next to the boat, said, 'Those bastards are shootin' at us.' The lady in the boat started screaming, 'WE'RE ALL GONNA DIE! WE'RE ALL GONNA DIE!' Her son had already jumped head-first out of the boat! We started yellin' that we were rescuers, and we were there to help them. I guess they didn't hear us.

"Then, BANG, BANG, BANG! again. So, we all jumped in the boat. Bill fired up the motor we got the hell out of there. As, soon as we were outta range, Bill pulled out his cell phone and called dispatch tellin' 'em what had happened and that we were done with that neighborhood!"

Jared was crew chief of this boat, and he was describing the only negative experience they had rescuing people. The overwhelming reaction from people they rescued was a sense of gratitude. Although there were lots of rumors floating around about rescue boats taking gunfire while working some neighborhoods, it was difficult finding a rescuer who had experienced such an incident. These types of interactions were few and far between during hurricane Harvey.

We'll never know if there was something shady going on in this case, or if it was just a case of cloudy or hazy vision. The people in the house may have mistaken the rescue crew for looters. The news media had reported looting stories.

It was getting dark. People still trapped in flooded homes felt left behind, alone and isolated. I can understand the agitated mental state of someone standing in water inside their home wouldn't be a model of clarity and calmness. This is what happens when we have a cloudy or hazy worldview window. With such a compromised worldview window, even the most innocent set of circumstances surrounding a relationship can seem threatening.

Gratitude is the currency of the universe. It opens and sustains relationships, no matter if those relationships are momentary or lifelong. A fleeting encounter with someone in need of your help could blossom into a relationship that thrusts you into your destiny. Treat everyone with kindness, dignity and respect. They may be that long-awaited key to unlocking your success.

Likewise, I can assure you that lifelong relationships are lubricated by gratitude. Spending a lifetime, or even a long time, with a spouse is neither an easy nor an effortless endeavor. It's made easier and requires less effort when the relationship is built on a mutual attitude of gratitude.

> For the few days this metropolitan area was under the magnifying glass of a curious world, **we demonstrated what a city full of goodness looks like.**

Houston is a city abounding in relationships build on thankful and grateful hearts. We are thankful to be a part of this great city, thankful for its can-do spirit, thankful for the opportunity to start over and thankful for a non-judgmental acceptance of who we are. I know I am. I wasn't born here, but I got here as quickly as I could. And, I couldn't be more grateful for the privilege of calling Houston my home.

For the few days this metropolitan area was under the magnifying glass of a curious world, **we demonstrated what a city full of goodness looks like.** We modeled ethical intelligence in action as only the largest city in Texas and, arguably, the most diverse city in the world, could. We provided a glimpse of what is possible, even now in our divided nation and contentious world.

Now, we look at another essential asset our city possesses, people who know, pursue, and find peace in their purpose.

CHAPTER 5

FINDING PEACE IN PURPOSE

Houston Police Sergeant Steve Perez's Funeral

He died as he lived, serving his fellow citizens. Sergeant Steve Perez of the Houston Police Department found his life's purpose in serving as a police officer. On August 29, 2017, while navigating flooded roads in darkness on his way to another 12-hour shift, Sergeant Perez mistakenly drove into an inundated freeway underpass. Struggling to exit his badly submerged and flooded vehicle, Sergeant Perez made the ultimate sacrifice, completing his earthly assignment as a dedicated public servant. At the funeral, his son said, "I know my dad is at peace."

Sergeant Steve Perez found peace in his life's purpose. You and I can, too. Everything and everyone has a purpose. We're not just a clump of differentiated atoms existing to absorb resources and eject waste. We are greater than the sum of our material parts. All of us are designed to serve a purpose greater than ourselves. No one else shares your purpose. It's personal to you. And only you are uniquely equipped to fulfill it. When you internalize this truth, jealousy and envy disappear from your life. You get to run your race. No one else can run it like you. Your purpose is a gift. Seek, discover and pursue it, and you'll find peace like Sergeant Perez.

This chapter is devoted to stories about people who found their purpose and lived it well during hurricane Harvey by serving others. Their stories show us how unique our purposes are and the joy that comes from their pursuit. Most of the stories you'll read in this chapter are about people whose names are familiar because they publicly serve our community in one way or another. As you'll see, combining your life's purpose with your "job" is wonderful to behold. We start with the water and a scenario related by Harris County Sheriff Ed Gonzalez.

Water, Water Everywhere

"We were over on 610 loop…the North Loop 610 at about north Wayside. Right around LBJ. It looked almost like a war-torn country. I saw people walking along the emergency lanes of the freeway. And, it had flooded down to the street level.

"I was with a crew of about five to six people. We spotted an individual on top of a fence holding on for dear life. The fence was maybe about 8 feet high. And the water was almost up to where he was. To rescue him, we had to form a human chain. We borrowed a hose from a Metro worker who happened to stop to help. Piecing that together and improvising

CHAPTER 5: FINDING PEACE IN PURPOSE

we were able to get in the water, in full uniform, and rescue the man.

"We came to find out that he was a security worker that had stayed at his post to the last moment. I remember thinking, I want him to work for me because I need that kind of commitment to the job. The rescued security worker said that he started work probably around eleven in the morning the prior day. He said that he had been up there on the fence since at least 2:00 AM.

Harris County Sheriff Ed Gonzalez

"He had stayed at his post. The water had risen to the point where he could not leave, and he was unable to swim. Even if he wanted to, the water was just so dirty and polluted. And, the current was tremendous. I clearly remember that because we were **in the current**. And, the water reached up to our necks! So, that rescue really set the tone."

> "...he was unable to swim. Even if he wanted to, the water was just so dirty and polluted. And, the current was tremendous. I clearly remember that because we were **in the current**. And, the water reached up to our necks!"

Leading in Wet Darkness. Ed Gonzalez, shown in the nearby photo, was responding to my question about his first encounter with rescue operations as hurricane Harvey reached the Houston area. Sheriff Gonzalez leads a law enforcement organization employing almost 5,000 officers and support personnel tasked with serving over four million residents in the third largest county in United States. He is also charged with leading and managing a modern jail facility housing more than 8,000 inmates. Yet, there he was. A CEO wearing a three-piece suit, in his case a full uniform, wading in neck-deep, dirty, polluted and fast-moving water in the middle of the night with his officers rescuing a stranger. And, did I mention, there was a hurricane packing high winds and driving horizonal rain moving through the area while this rescue was happening? Sheriff Gonzalez wasn't in that water because it was his job. No, he was in that water because serving, saving and helping is his life's purpose! It also happens to be his job! We should all be so blessed. Then, we have the life-threatening water facility story no one heard about! Until now, that is, as told by Houston Mayor Sylvester Turner.

> Yet, there he was. A CEO wearing a three-piece suit, in his case a full uniform, wading in neck-deep, dirty, polluted and fast moving water in the middle of the night with his officers rescuing a complete stranger.

> "One of the critical moments was on Monday morning after three rain bands came through on Sunday night carrying seven to nine inches of rain each. [That would be 21 to 27 inches] The city was inundated. Jeff, the acting public works director and his deputy came to me and said the Northeast Water Purification plant, our largest, was under water, and it was going to cease functioning in about three hours, which meant we were going to have to order water boiling.
>
> "That prospect was greatly concerning. Jeff told me about the problem about 9 o'clock that morning. At that time, we were having press conferences twice a day, at morning and midnight, and the last thing I wanted to do was to report that

the water was not usable, which would have greatly added to everyone's anxiety.

"So I told Jeff, 'if you are saying to me is that you all have tried everything, and you've talked to everybody, both within the city as well as consultants and companies outside of the city, and if you all have concluded that there's nothing else we can do to keep the plant operational, then I will make the announcement that the people will have to boil the water.'"

I want to interrupt the Mayor's story for a quick observation. I hope you see, as I did, the extraordinary efforts Mayor Turner was making so that he could tell the public the truth. Most politicians wouldn't worry about it. The Mayor continued.

"But before I make that pronouncement you will need to tell me there is nothing else that anybody can do. So, what I would ask you is, 'if you're not in a position to say that, then go back and talk to more people—certainly this is not the first time that a water plant has been underwater—so talk with as many experts and others, whether inside or outside the city. And, at this moment, money is not an object! So, whatever it will take to keep the water system functioning then let's do it.'

"So, they went off. I had a press conference, and I alerted people that we were having problems at the Northeast Water Purification plant—that it was underwater. I reported we were doing everything that we could to make sure that the plant was functional and that I would let people know later on what additional steps might have to be taken.

"At about one o'clock that afternoon, Jeff came back to me and said that they had reached out to some other experts and

thought that they had bought us an additional eight hours. I said, "fine." 'Let's keep working. Just keep doing whatever you need to do to keep that plant up and running. And again, money is not an object! Whatever it takes to keep it going, keep it going'.

"And, then Jeff came back to me later on that evening and said, 'I think we can keep the plant going for another day.' I said, 'Fine. Let's keep it going.' Then on Tuesday late afternoon Jeff came to me and said Mayor, 'It will stay up'. His team had put in place a bypass system that was able to keep the entire plant operational.

> 'Let's keep working. Just keep doing whatever you need to do to keep that plant up and running. And again, money is not an object! Whatever it takes to keep it going, keep it going'

"That's when, this huge weight lifted off my shoulders. It was a major relief. We were talking about a water system that impacted millions of people who were trapped in their homes. So, knowing that the plant was going to stay up and functioning and that I didn't have to tell people to boil water, was a big plus. After that, as far as I was concerned, everything else was, well, highly manageable! Then, we had this problem."

As I listened to Mayor Turner calmly relate these tense circumstances, I thought back to the conversation I'd had with Chief Acevedo where he offered some philosophical musings about Mayor Turner's election. Chief Acevedo said he believed Mayor Turner had been elected for a time such as this, a time that required the mayor's calm and reassuring leadership. Mayor Turner continued his story.

"We had two wastewater treatment facilities, Turkey Creek and West Avenue that were under water and presented the prospect of waste water backing up into people's homes, again homes they couldn't leave. We employed the same method. Whatever we need to do to make sure that the systems worked. Both were totally submerged, but we ended up working with other outside companies to fix the problem.

"We put in an above-ground-four-mile bypass system of pipes for the West Avenue wastewater facility. And, then, we also put in some portable systems that served as a bypass and kept West Avenue functioning. And that made sure that the wastewater did not back up into people's homes. And it worked, so that was another big relief. Everything else then became highly manageable."

A Mayor's Mayor. The preceding was Sylvester Turner, as shown in the nearby photo, dispassionately responding, in the business-like-low-key manner I've just related, to my question, "What was your darkest moment during the hurricane event?" After hearing his answer, I was a bit surprised.

I had expected a far different response, one that was a bit more, shall we say, "glamorous" and excitedly covered by the news media. Something like, "It was when I learned that we had firefighters wading in waist deep water rescuing people only to find out the water was electrified because the power was still on. When the firefighters reported they could feel the electricity coursing through their legs, we had to pull them out of the water." Or,

"It was when that tornado went up I-45 and tore the roofs off flooded apartments and condominiums in the Greenspoint area. We had to muster an immediate air, water and ground response." Both of those more "glamorous" incidents did occur and were handled amazingly well by first responders and others. But, Mayor Turner was laser-focused on running his race, maintaining the overall safety and well-being of **all** the millions of people who live in the city of Houston.

Mayor Sylvester Turner leads the city government of Houston, Texas, the fourth largest and soon the third largest city in the country. The Houston city limits encompass an area of about 627 square miles with an estimated 2017 population of 2.5 million people, growing by more than 2,400 new arrivals per week. The Mayor's team consists of more than 20 leaders whose departments employ over 20,000 people. His knowing-your-life's-purpose leadership is one of the reasons Houston is rapidly recovering from the ravages of hurricane Harvey.

Flooded Greenspoint Apartment Complex

One of the many benefits of knowing and pursuing your life's purpose is that it helps you run **your** life's race. You have the unique combination of talent, skills and tools to run your race. No one else has exactly that same combination. One of the reasons we fail, is that we've jumped into someone's else's race where we're not well equipped for success in that arena. Both Sheriff Gonzalez and Mayor Turner showed us how it's done. Here's another shining example from Chief Acevedo.

> "I remember being with my officers on Saturday night, the night that the rain and wind really hit hard. We had almost immediate flooding in the Meyerland area. We had flooding in the Greenspoint area, as shown in the nearby photo. We had flooding all over the place. I joined my officers at Greenspoint that night close to rapidly rising Greens Bayou. When we got there, I started doing rescues with them because I lead from the front, and I wanted to get a sense of the operational challenges we were facing.
>
> "I was new to Houston. I had never experienced flooding here in Houston. I remember when I first got to the Greenspoint area, I was up to my knees in water rescuing people from those apartment complexes. By the time we were done, we were waist deep in water. The water was rising that fast! And, it was still pouring rain!
>
> "My thoughts about Harvey when it hit and as we were living through it, was amazement at the amount of destruction and the power of the water. Something that was of a historical nature that in recorded history we hadn't experienced.

The weather channel had to create a new color, I think it was purple that they chose. I say it was symbolic for the fact that we were bruised and beaten up pretty well."

As I watched chief Acevedo relate this story, I was struck by how passionately he loved and respected the people he led. One of the cardinal rules of leadership is that the people you lead must know you respect and care about them. Chief Acevedo is an exemplary figure in that regard. He continued praising his people.

"I was amazed I saw police officers doing things I've never seen police officers do, especially in the numbers of incidents we handled. The respect that I have and love for this organization called the Houston Police Department is unparalleled. I love police officers. I love policing. I loved the California Highway Patrol. I loved the Austin Police Department. But, these men and women—I've fallen in love with them because of their can-do attitude. Just think about law enforcement's job.

"I'll never forget my homicide crew. All of them were in the back of a pickup truck. It was pouring down rain. The wind was howling."

"We're not a rescue organization. We're a safety organization. And I saw my department, my men and women, upholding their public safety responsibilities, maintaining law and order. But, they also took on rescue missions, and that is not normally what we do. I'll never forget my homicide crew. All of them were in the back of a pickup truck. It was pouring down rain. The wind was howling. And there they were packed in the back of that truck, about 20 of them. I said, 'Hey crazies, where're you going?' They said, 'Chief we hear they're some rescues that need to happen. We're gonna go rescue people.'

> "The things I saw these men and women do, all without being equipped or trained, was amazing. Their collective heart, not just of our cops but of the citizens and residents that we serve and the communities that responded to, restored in me—I don't want to say restored—I've never lost faith in humanity, but it strengthened my resolve and my belief that as much ugliness as there is in the world, human beings, by and large, are pretty special people. Humans are just special creatures."

Loving The People You Lead. Houston Police Chief, Art Acevedo, was describing one of the hundreds of his hurricane Harvey experiences in a short but wide-ranging interview. From the moment we began talking, it was obvious this man was living his life's purpose. He loves policing. He always has. Here was the CEO of a 5,000-person organization. He could have been sitting in his office wearing a more comfortable civilian suit. But, he wasn't. Chief Acevedo was in full uniform ready to go on an emergency call at a moment's notice. He loves his life's work, and it happens to be his job.

Chief Acevedo is a 21st century leader. He not only understands servant leadership, but he's also instinctually becoming a gardener, a leader raising more leaders. When I consult with organizations helping their leadership teams enhance their skills, I like to talk to team members, some call them followers, to get their perspectives. I had a serendipitous opportunity in this instance.

Shortly after I interviewed the Chief, I happened to be riding in a downtown office building elevator with a uniformed Houston police officer. I offhandedly mentioned that I had recently talked to his boss who told me that he likes to lead from the front. The police officer got a smile on his face and said "Yes, I've seen more of him [Chief Acevedo] in the short time he's been here than I saw the prior two chiefs the entire time they led the department."

We'll talk more about Chief Acevedo in Chapter 8. Let's consider one more example of knowing and living your life's purpose from Perryn Leech, Managing Director of the Houston Grand Opera. I interviewed Director Leech because his public reaction to hurricane Harvey's aftermath seemed to indicate a man who knew his purpose in life.

> *"It's important to know the background I come from. My dad was a doctor and wanted me to be a doctor. Luckily, I have a very, very intelligent elder sister. So, she kinda got the majority of the sort of 'doctor' thing, smarts and…. What I loved doing was playing sports and doing theater. That's two intersections that normally aren't in sync very much. So, I was in a group of one who was in both of those camps, playing a lot of sports rugby, cricket and football and doing lots of arts and drama. The school I went to just had that in its mix. Those were the two things I enjoyed doing, not so much the academics stuff. I didn't like that all that much.*
>
> *"So, when I said I wanted to go to drama school and study theater, which is where my interests were, my mum was very supportive. My dad was like, 'You've got to get a proper job. We've spent a huge amount of money on your education. Why would you not get a job where you can actually earn some money.' I could understand that. So, the majority of my friends went off to work in the city and other things. So, I went to drama school. I enjoyed it very much."*

Director Leech painted a portrait of the rare student who knows exactly what he wants to do with his life. Over the course of my teaching career, I've had thousands of students in my classrooms. Most of them had no idea where they were going in life. I silently wondered how the world would change if more of our students had this level of self-knowledge at such an early age. Director Leech continued.

> "I got a job straight out of drama school at the Glyndebourne Festival, which is a big opera festival in the U. K., and, then, I started freelancing. One of the important things my dad, and my mum, taught me was a work ethic. You're only as good as the last day you worked. So, nothing you've done in the past ever matters. It's only what you do the next day. I think that's stood me in pretty good stead as I carried on in my career.
>
> "So, for 15 to 16 years I did this freelance theatre career in which some years I was working 72 to 73 weeks because I had jobs that overlapped. My accountant was like, 'You're a nightmare because you've got 76 weeks of work here. How am I supposed to put you on a tax return?' I told him, 'That's why I pay you!'
>
> "So, I've always been like that. As a freelancer that worked very well. I was always available. I'd end one job, and, then, have to drive 400 miles overnight to start the next job first thing in the morning. Sometimes I had two jobs going at the same time. I was always busy. People loved my work. I did it because I loved what I was doing!"

> "You're only as good as the last day you worked. So, nothing you've done in the past ever matters. It's only what you do the next day."

Keeping the Artists Happy and the Stage Ready. Director Perryn Leech, was describing how he got into his life's work.

From a very early age, Director Leech, began living his life's purpose—making it possible for live audiences to enjoy great theatrical productions. He was fortunate in that he had a family who supported him and the personal self-confidence and drive to step out and do something that many considered not a "proper" job. Many of us lack the courage to embark upon such a bold initiative.

Discovering and pursuing your life's purpose is an important element of an ethically intelligent life. These four leaders show that truth with the way they live their lives. With leaders like this, perhaps, it's why the people in this community displayed such an ethically intelligent response to hurricane Harvey and its aftermath. Incidentally, I'll let your question about why I interviewed Director Leech go unanswered until Chapter 10. Now we turn to the news media and Nikki Courtney and Scott Crowder, KTRH NewsRadio Anchors and Reporters.

Calm Before, During and After

> "We're back! Continuing with our Storm Team coverage of hurricane Harvey. I'm Nikki Courtney with my partner, Scott Crowder, and we're here until 5:00 today. Doppler Radar shows heavy rain continuing throughout the Houston area. We're here for you, folks! (Nikki and Scott are pictured at the station during the storm in the photo nearby.)
>
> "In addition to bringing you the latest updates from the mayor and other officials, I want this afternoon to be about you. We're all stressed. And if I get a little emotional on you, please know we're all feeling the pain of this ongoing disaster. Now, we're opening the phone lines so that you can call in with your stories, needs or if you just need to talk."

Nikki: *"Our first caller is Jim from Katy. Hello Jim! What's it like in your neighborhood?"*

Jim: *"It's still rainin' pretty hard here, but the streets in our neighborhood are passable. You asked for stories of people helping each other. I wanted to tell the story of the guy who owns the company I work for. Several of my coworkers have been flooded out of their homes. My boss has been trying to help all of them. In one case, he got his RV, parked it in his driveway, and let Betty and her family move into the RV until they get their home repaired. It was such a great gesture on his part, I just wanted to tell everybody about it. Thanks for the opportunity to call in."*

Scott Crowder and Nikki Courtney

Nikki: *"What a great story! Thank you, Jim. "Our second caller is Raymond from Kingwood. Hello Raymond! How can we help you?"*

Raymond: *'We need help out here!'*

Nikki: *"What kind of help?"*

Raymond: *"The flooding is real bad. We're rescuin' people and takin' 'em to the Second Baptist church on Park Drive. The church is full of rescued people. They need more volunteers and supplies."*

Nikki: *"Thank you Raymond. Well, you heard it folks. The Second Baptist church on Park Drive in Kingwood needs supplies and volunteers. Now we have Pearl from Northeast Houston on the line. What's on your mind, Pearl?"*

Pearl: *"I'm scared! I'm retired, and I live alone. I need a walker to get around. It's rainin' so hard, and water's startin' to come in under my back door. What should I do?"*

Nikki: *"Pearl, it's gonna be alright! Just stay calm. We're gonna get you some help. Just stay on the line. I'll be right back. Folk's, Mayor Turner and Judge Emmett are giving an update. We're gonna go to them right now."*

So, it went. Hour after hour. Day after day. Nikki Courtney, Scott Crowder and all their colleagues at KTRH NewsRadio reported on the storm. Nikki lived at the station for five days, sleeping on Michael Berry's couch, as shown in the nearby photo.  She and her colleagues were a lifeline to the community, dispensing information, knowledge, kindness, comfort and solace to thousands, especially those who were alone like Pearl. For me, and many other listeners, Nikki Courtney was the "Voice of the Storm."

During my career, first in business and then in higher education, I've met and worked with thousands of people. One observation I can make, without any reservation, is that people who are living their purpose and pursuing what they were "born to do" were the happiest and most fulfilled people. And, it didn't matter what that "born to do" was.

I've known many top business executives like that. Even accounting for 60-to-80-hour-work weeks and long stints away from family, they loved what they did and didn't want to do anything else. Even after mandatory retirement age forced them from their organization, these executives found other ways to continue their work. Their attitude was, "if you love what you're doing, why quit?"

CHAPTER 5: FINDING PEACE IN PURPOSE

I recently had my car serviced, and I was talking to one of the service technicians. He told me how he'd always loved cars and spent countless hours working on them for free. He related how he loved getting his hands dirty transforming something that didn't work into something that did. He said he'd never considered doing any other kind of work.

Radio people seem a bit more certain about their life's purpose than most. Over the years, I have had the occasion to speak with many people in the radio business. Most of them related how the business was a special calling, and that "they just knew" it early in life. Scott Crowder. KTRH NewsRadio Anchor and Reporter. told me, "I've always been a radio guy. I started out behind the scenes and eventually became an on-air personality."

Love him or hate him, Rush Limbaugh is the biggest name in AM talk radio. He's been heard many times saying something like, "Radio is all I ever wanted to do. I knew at age 13 that I wanted radio to be my life." I could cite many other examples, but I think you get the point. Nikki Courtney is a special "Harvey" instance of living your life purpose.

> "I've always approached radio—we're all about being silly and stupid, we laugh and carry on and have fun—but when the shit hits the fan, we save lives."

> *"Harvey hit two weeks before my 40th anniversary in radio. When I started in radio, I had to take an oath that committed me to being a public servant. And, that as a broadcaster I was assuming the responsibility, that in times of crisis we would serve the public. I took that to be a duty and responsibility. I've always approached radio—we're all about being silly and stupid, we laugh and carry on and have fun—but when the shit hits the fan, we save lives.*
>
> *"Tone of voice is everything. Don't ever let your voice go*

up. Don't let your voice go shrill. I have a deep voice, when I don't have a cold. My rule is keep your voice down. Hurricane Harvey coverage was just that—very much about the tone of voice.

"After 911, there was a panel on CSPAN. Brokaw, Rather, Jennings and Blitzer were the panelists talking about 911, and what it was like being a journalist during that event. One of them said, 'you know its oddest thing, but the thought that I kept coming back to that day was to really monitor my tone of voice.' And everybody physically turned and went, 'YES!!'

"I was sitting there watching it on television going. YES. I think what we learned on that day was how you say things is almost as important as what you say. I think, more than anything else, during Harvey, for me, was trying to remember to be calm and reassuring. I kept telling myself, 'We can do this—project an air of confidence and reassurance.'"

She succeeded! Hour after hour, and day after day. For eleven 24/7-days, Nikki and her colleagues at KTRH NewsRadio projected an air of reassurance, confidence and a sense of well-being that may or may not have been exactly what was going on behind the scenes. It was, in my opinion, a stellar example of the news media fulfilling their purpose in our society. We witnessed a display of purity of purpose not often seen these days, especially from "the Media." Lisa Shumate, Associate Vice President and General Manager, Houston Public Media agreed.

Purity of Purpose Rarely Seen

"I think the Houston media did an extraordinary job covering hurricane Harvey. I've seen the media cover hurricane Ike. I've

CHAPTER 5: FINDING PEACE IN PURPOSE

seen the media cover Katrina. I've grown up and lived in the south my whole life, and I've been in media for a very long time. So, as a media person, you know what you're up against when these storms get into the Gulf. You pack a bag, and you're not sure when you're going to get back home.

"When you see events like Katrina and Ike and Harvey, where there is human suffering. suffering from the stress of the flooding, the volume of the flooding, being stranded and homeless, it takes a real toll on the media community. I just think everybody was extremely professional and really focused on trying to help people. I give the media very high marks."

> We tend to forget that behind those microphones and cameras is someone just like us. Humans who have aunts, uncles, spouses and best friends. They hurt and cry.

Lisa Shumate was giving me her professional assessment of the news media's performance during hurricane Harvey. She was also reminding all of us non-media types of the emotional toll covering an event like hurricane Harvey takes on members of the media.

We tend to forget that behind those microphones and cameras is someone just like us. Humans who have aunts, uncles, spouses and best friends. They hurt and cry. They have good days and bad. They are dedicated to their jobs. They make mistakes. Don't we all?

We love to hate the media. Our fragmented culture asks, no compels, us to take sides. Too many of us have affirmatively answered culture's call. Unfortunately, many members of the media also have not only taken a side but let that bias infect their work. Is that part of the news media's purpose? Let's explore, focusing on the local Houston news media.

The "Press," as an institution, is protected by our constitution. For simplicity's sake I'm using the term "Press" very expansively, and I'm conflating journalism with the news media. I know that's not necessarily true. And, I'm mixing apples and oranges, but it's not important in this instance.

The American Press Institute defines the following as the **purpose** of journalism, aka the news media:

> The purpose of journalism is thus to provide citizens with the information they need to make the best possible decisions about their lives, their communities, their societies, and their governments. News is that part of communication that keeps us informed of the changing events, issues, and characters in the world outside. Though it may be interesting or even entertaining, the foremost value of news is as a utility to empower the informed.

Houston is a large media market. We have hundreds of media outlets, all of whom provided some level of coverage of hurricane Harvey and its aftermath. I reached out to several of these outlets. Only one responded, iHeart Media. That was a bit serendipitous because I happen to listen to iHeart's Houston AM radio stations, especially during significant news events when the electrical power is offline. So, I'm not playing favorites, just recognizing the adage, "90% of success in life is just showing up." iHeart showed up.

Bryan Erickson, Director of AM Programming for iHeartMedia in Houston said the following about their storm coverage.

> "Our attitude towards storm coverage is simple—**we're here to serve the community**—whatever it takes. [Bolding is mine]

"We have a Hurricane Season Plan in place, which we implement each year a couple of weeks before hurricane season starts in June. It's a comprehensive plan that covers all seven stations in our Houston iHeart cluster. It spells out duties and responsibilities not just for the news staff, but for our support staff, our sales team, our traffic and continuity staff and our engineering and IT teams.

> "Our attitude towards storm coverage is simple—**we're here to serve the community**—whatever it takes."

"The plan also includes partnering with other iHeart stations in nearby cities to augment our coverage, or their coverage, as needed. We started our live non-stop coverage of Harvey about eight hours before we had planned to because our stations in Corpus Christi got knocked off the air. We wanted to make sure people in that region were getting the latest information.

Our plan also includes making sure our staff has a personal disaster plan in place for their own families. Most of the staff will be here at the stations before, during and after a storm hits and won't be able to be with their families. We want to make sure their needs have been taken care of before a storm enters the region."

Director Erickson was responding to my question about storm coverage attitudes. Echoing the definition of news media purpose, I cited above, He continued,

"Making sure we were disseminating the most important and timely information at any given moment was a constant challenge. The scale of the disaster was so large we continually asked ourselves if we were covering everything in every area *affected. There was just so much information and it was coming in constantly.*

"We spent a great deal of our broadcast time doing live interviews with area officials, first responders and storm victims, many of them dealing with what was the most devastating event of their lives. Despite what they were going through, so many of them took the time to express their gratitude for our coverage. It felt strange because the people who deserved gratitude were the people we were talking too— the first responders and regular folks who spent countless hours coming to the aid of their neighbors.

"Part of our information challenge was how to handle what we were seeing on social media. There was a constant stream of information coming in on Twitter and Facebook and, as we've all discovered, it's not always easy to separate fact from fiction. Social media is an amazing tool when it comes to connecting with our audience—they can reach out to us like never before. How we use that information is a challenge that all media organizations will continue to face daily."

I hope you see the same commitment to purpose I see in those words. You see an organization and its people committed to finding and reporting the truth to the public in their actions as well as words. Lest you think staying true to this commitment was easy, let's revisit the scene.

"I knew at that moment that I had to rise to the challenge. With my signs and notes in hand, I went to the control room

and physically kicked the door because I was going to go take charge. We had a hurricane. It was coming in to Corpus. We didn't know how Houston was going to be threatened yet. But I had lives to save. I had a duty to perform. The army brat that I am I wanted to be up for the challenge. I went in with confidence, with conviction, and I kicked the door in, ready to go!"

That was Nikki Courtney describing her preparation for kicking off storm coverage that August Friday when hurricane Harvey made landfall in Rockport, Texas. In that statement, you see a level of courage and commitment from behind the scenes news consumers rarely see. Critics might say, "Yeah, but she's old school. What about these young people coming into the business?" My answer, Brandi Smith.

KHOU 11 News reporter Brandi Smith and her photojournalist partner, Mario Sandoval, took over the KHOU broadcast when the station and studio were flooded. The Smith/Sandoval team, then, went on to help rescue an eighteen-wheeler driver trapped in his truck by flagging down a Harris County Sheriff's department rescue team. The truck driver credited the team's work with saving his life.

That wasn't the only instance of members of the news media helping save lives during hurricane Harvey. There were many others. The point is that the dedication to living your life's purpose is alive and well in the news media. As we complete this chapter about finding peace in your life purpose, I give you one last quote from Nikki Courtney.

In this quote, she was reflecting on how short-handed the station was and how emotionally drained the staff was because of Matt Patrick's tragic death, after an heroic struggle with cancer, just a few weeks earlier. Matt was a very popular and beloved co-host of the KTRH Houston's Morning News Show with Shara Fryer. His passing was a major event for the iHeart Houston family.

> *"With duct tape, baling wire, magic and mirrors, Bryan Erickson kept this radio station on the air. As a listener, you probably don't even think about what goes on behind the microphone. For example, that commercial saying "Give to the Red Cross" or anything about Harvey ... somebody had to write it and, then, get it to a person that voices it, who, then, gets it to a producer who produces it and assigns a number to it and, then, gets it on the air.*
>
> *"All those functions have to be done by somebody. There are a million little nuts and bolts that go into keeping a radio station on the air and functioning. And through all of it, Bryan and Marc and the management team, unlike anything I've ever experienced,* **kept us going.***"*

We began this chapter recounting Steve Perez's death serving the community as a police officer, a service that he saw as his purpose in life. We can never know for sure, but those closest to him believed that community service brought Sergeant Perez internal peace. We then considered several other community leaders and organizations noting how they found personal satisfaction in pursuing their purposes. This, **I firmly believe is the truth of the universe—pursuing your purpose in life brings peace to your mind and spirit.**

We now turn from simply keeping going to going in the right direction under the guidance of our internal compass.

CHAPTER 6

KNOWING AND DOING RIGHT

Grandmother Teaching Her Grandson Values – Forming His Internal Compass

"Grammy, I'm goin' out!" yelled young Josh.

"NO! You're NOT! It's still rainin'. Harvey is still sittin' over us. And, the street's underwater!" yelled Maria, Josh's grandmother.

"Grammy, my friends are waitin' on me! I gotta go. I'll be back before dark!"

With that rejoinder, Josh scooted out the front door of Maria's modest two-bedroom home, located in one of Houston's oldest neighborhoods.

Maria began raising Josh when he was five. Maria's daughter, Josh's mother Elena, died in an auto accident. Josh's dad disappeared when Josh was two and hasn't been seen since. Maria still works part-time as a bookkeeper, trying to be home when Josh comes home from school. Because her home is paid off, Josh and Maria have a comfortable but basic lifestyle.

Just before dark, Josh bounded through the front door soaked to the skin but wearing a new hoodie and carrying a pair of stylish running shoes. Maria rushed into the kitchen, looked at Josh and demanded,

"Where'd you get those shoes? And, whose, hoodie is that?" Josh triumphantly said,

"I found 'em floatin' down the street!" Maria retorted,

"Oh Yeah! I'm gonna ask you one more time. Where'd you get those shoes? And, don't tell me NO MORE lies!" Josh had heard that voice before. It's the voice his Grammy got when she was spittin' mad. Staring down at the floor, Josh mumbled,

"I got 'em at Tal's store. We were wadin' by the store. The water was up to our knees, and the door was busted in. There were lots of folks goin' in and out. So, we went in just to look around. It was dark 'n the place was trashed. The stuff was all wet 'n ruined. So, we decided we could pick somethin' out since it was just gonna be thrown away anyway.

There was a long silence. Maria thought to herself, **He's had a hard life. He never knew his dad. His mother is a faint distant memory. The gangs in the neighborhood were hard at work trying to recruit him. I can't afford to buy him nice things.** Maria broke the silence,

"Josh, you can't just take someone's stuff without askin'." Josh said,

"But, it's all wet and ruined!" Remaining calm, Maria replied,

CHAPTER 6: KNOWING AND DOING RIGHT

"It's not ruined enough for you not to want it, is it?" Josh mumbled,

"No." Maria continued,

"Taking someone's property without permission or paying for it, isn't right. You just can't do it! We don't live that way!" Josh, meekly said,

"Yes, Grammy." Maria continued,

"As soon as the rain stops and the water goes down, we're gonna return the shoes and hoodie to Tal's place and you're gonna apologize." With a bit of fear in his voice, Josh protested,

"But he's gonna be real mad that his placed is trashed! Suppose he turns me in to the police?" Maria replied,

"It's a little late to think of that now! No! You're gonna face the consequences. You're gonna do the right thing!"

> My mother's role, in most cases, was to simply tell me, "You just wait until your father gets home! He'll take care of this!"

As a youth, this kind of story was a more common part of my life experience than I'd care to admit. Except, in my case it was my father exchanging the dialogue with me. My mother's role, in most cases, was to simply tell me, "You just wait until your father gets home! He'll take care of this!" That statement always filled me with a kind of dread because my father was, shall we say, serious about taking care of whatever "this" was. But, I learned right from wrong.

The right from wrong I learned came from the common worldview shared in the Midwest United States in the late 1940s and early 1950s, perhaps, leavened by my father's Romanian and my mother's Polish upbringing and tinged with the teachings of the Romanian Orthodox and Roman Catholic churches. Like it or not, this is how our Internal Compass is formed.

Our Internal Compass is the arbiter of our beliefs about what's right and what's wrong. It's formed early in our lives and reflects the worldview of the community in which we're raised. Our Internal Compass determines our true North—referred to in various ways, including such phrases, "finding the right", "determining the right thing to do", "doing right", "staying on the right path" or "living righteously." Finding a common true North, however, is neither simple nor easy.

Finding True North

As part of my organizational culture, ethics and ethical intelligence research, I've conducted hundreds of experiential interviews with people. In those interviews, without exception, people profess an earnest desire to do right, using many of the common phrases I just mentioned. And, I believed them.

Their sincerity was never in doubt. The problem is everyone's true North is not the same. Mine may point in one direction. Yours may be slightly different than mine or, it could be radically different, depending on where we grew up. What's that? Oh, you're wondering what this has to do with Houston and hurricane Harvey. Just stick with me. We'll get there momentarily.

Recently, I read an article written by Karin McQuillan, a former Peace Corps volunteer. Her experience provides an insightful description of how different worldviews determine where our Internal Compass points. Here's a mosaic of snippets taken from her article.

CHAPTER 6: KNOWING AND DOING RIGHT

Three weeks after college, I flew to Senegal, West Africa, to run a community center in a rural town. As a twenty-one-year-old starting out in the Peace Corps, I loved Senegal. In fact, I was euphoric. I quickly made friends and had an adopted family. I relished the feeling of the brotherhood of man. People were open, willing to share their lives and, after they knew you, their innermost thoughts.

The longer I lived there, the more I understood: it became blindingly obvious that the Senegalese are not the same as us. The truths we hold to be self-evident are not evident to the Senegalese. Take something as basic as family. Family was a few hundred people, extending out to second and third cousins. All the men in one generation were called "father." Yet family was crucial to people there in a way Americans cannot comprehend.

The Ten Commandments were not disobeyed—they were unknown. The value system was the exact opposite. You were supposed to steal everything you can to give to your own relatives. All the little stores in Senegal were owned by Mauritanians. If a Senegalese wanted to run a little store, he'd go to another country. The reason? Your friends and relatives would ask you for stuff for free, and you would have to say yes. End of your business. You are not allowed to be a selfish individual and say no to relatives.

I've never been to Senegal, and I can't vouch for the truth of Ms. McQuillan's commentary. But, I've been in business for many decades. I've either been a member of or consulted with large multinational organizations. And, I've traveled and lived overseas.

I can tell you, without a doubt, that people around the world have starkly diverse views of what's right and what's wrong. This diversity of true ethical North has broad implications that I've written about elsewhere. The reason I raise this issue here is because I want to make a point about Houston and its response to the ravages of hurricane Harvey.

Houston is the most diverse city in the United States and, perhaps, the world. I won't regale you with the supporting facts and statistics. I listed them earlier in this book. If ever there was a place where you would expect to find endless conflict about what's right and what's wrong, you would expect to find it in a metropolitan area with such a multiplicity of worldviews as Houston. **We don't, and we didn't!**

We don't have endless conflict here, despite our differences, because we respect one another. This is a place where we truly practice Namasté—I acknowledge either your humanness or the same divine spirit that lives in me lives in you. Many of us have never heard of Namasté or don't know what it means, but we live it out every day, anyway. That's just us.

Here's a typical example of what I mean. On the surface, Mayor Sylvester Turner and I probably wouldn't agree on much politically. When I met him in December, I was not only grateful for his time but also impressed with his intellect, courage and leadership. Contrary to many of his critics, I think he did extraordinarily well during hurricane Harvey, and I believe he's administering the city efficiently and effectively. And, no! I don't think he should've told us to evacuate!

If I was abiding by the "national it's us against them" standard, I should be critical, demeaning and stand against anything Mayor Turner does simply

> If ever there was a place where you would expect to find endless conflict about what's right and what's wrong, you would expect to find it in a metropolitan area with such a multiplicity of worldviews as Houston. **We don't, and we didn't!**

because he isn't a member of my tribe, whatever tribe that is. No, that isn't us! We don't act like that here. In that respect, Houstonians, and I use that term geographically broadly, are Jeffersonians— "if what you do neither breaks my leg nor picks my pocket", I don't care. You might call it a live and let live attitude.

We saw this attitude at its finest during Houston's response to hurricane Harvey and its aftermath. We were kind, good, loving, respectful, helpful and nonjudgmental. Skin color, hair length, no hair, beards, no beards, accent, no accent, clothing, or not, uniform, or not, weight, height, high income, low income or no income, it didn't matter. We responded. We did what was right. Our Internal Compasses were in sync on the meaning of true North. If you were in trouble or needed help, we helped, as in the following story from Thad and Cindy!

> Houstonians, and I use that term geographically broadly, are Jeffersonians— "if what you do neither breaks my leg nor picks my pocket", I don't care. You might call it a live and let live attitude.

"My wife and I were doing what everyone said we shouldn't, we were out driving on the flooded streets. We were on the way to her mother's house. Cindy's mother lives by herself in, what I would consider a less than desirable neighborhood. Her husband, Fred, passed away a few years ago.

"We live in an area that we were pretty sure wouldn't flood, So, we decided to ride the storm out at her mother's place. I felt confident that our SUV was high enough to avoid getting stuck in any water. Wow! Was I wrong! Just when we exited the freeway near Kay's neighborhood, we drove right into high water on the feeder road. It was dark, no lights of any kind. From the freeway, we couldn't see that the feeder was flooded. And, even as we approached the end of the exit ramp,

the water didn't look more than a few inches deep.

"It was also pouring rain, and the windshield wipers couldn't keep the windshield clear enough to see. I slammed on the brakes so that we wouldn't hit the water at high speed. I was only partially successful. I finally slowed down to about three or four miles per hour. Then, I saw all the abandoned cars over by the curb, water midway up the doors. I was determined that we wouldn't stall out.

"So I kept driving as fast as I thought the car could handle. It kept getting deeper and deeper. Suddenly, the water was up over the doors and the engine died. I looked over at Cindy, and I could see fear and panic in her eyes. It was obvious we were in big trouble.

"As, we were trying to figure out how to get out of the car, I heard this loud rapping on the back window. A voice yelled, 'Do you need help?' Without thinking, I yelled, 'Yes, we'll take all the help we can get.' Two guys seemed to come out of nowhere wearing head mounted flashlights. They helped Cindy get out of the car. I quickly followed suit.

"The water was up to my waist, and it was so dark I couldn't tell which direction we should go. Fear and panic suddenly overcame my senses. It was like we were in an ocean that was getting deeper, and we couldn't see the shore. The two guys had an inflatable rubber raft and told us to grab hold of it. In the pitch darkness, they led us to safety.

> "It wasn't until several hours later in the rescue center, that I reflected on the two guys that helped us. One was a tall black guy with a thick accent. The other was wearing a turban and had a long black beard. At the time they were helping us, I never noticed those details. Of course, it was dark and hard to see. But, usually, I would notice those kinds of things. On that night it never occurred to me, and if it had, it wouldn't have made any difference."

I'm happy to report that Thad and Cindy's experience that night wasn't unique. I could've written a thousand-page book containing stories like this one. Even though Thad and Cindy were successful, young, white and well-dressed professionals driving an $80,000 SUV, it didn't matter to the two guys with the rubber raft. They were there to help, not pass judgment or personally profit from the circumstances. The two guys just did what was right. We saw their ethical intelligence in action.

When I spoke to Chief Acevedo, I asked him about crime during the Harvey emergency. In most crisis situations, like Harvey's flooding, we typically see outbreaks of looting and other types of crimes. Chief Acevedo said, "Starting Saturday night we had the entire department working and we saw very little looting. As a result we were able to affect thousands of rescues."

He went on, "In other natural disasters there are often reports of looting by law enforcement. I think we acquitted ourselves superbly. There wasn't even hint of a rumor about law enforcement engaging in that type of behavior." No, I didn't miss the news reports about looting and price gouging. I saw them, but such reports were few and far between, especially when compared to other emergencies.

Lest you think I am some type of sheltered individual who

has a Pollyannaish outlook on life, there were some among us who strayed outside of their ethical comfort zone. We'll consider that comfort zone and the Ethical Fence that determines it now. Here's a recent encounter I had with a foundation contractor.

Ethical Comfort Zone

"I've finished my evaluation. I've drawn a diagram of your house, and I've taken several dozen elevation readings. As I think you already know just by looking around inside your house, you have a cracked slab. Cracks in the walls and in the ceiling inside the house are the result of the northeast corner of your house sinking towards the cul-de-sac.

"The good news is, we won't have to jackhammer holes in the floor inside the house. We can confine our work to the outside. I am recommending that we install 16 piers around the front of your house. Using those piers, we can lift your house back into its proper level position.

"We'll have to dig up all of the shrubs around the outside of the house. And, we'll have to excavate the gas and water lines coming into the house so that when we lift the house we don't damage those lines. I'm estimating that we can get this work done in one long workday. Our estimate for the cost is"—**a whole lot of money!**

My foundation contractor was providing me an oral report of his evaluation of my house foundation. My house is located next to the man-made lake in our subdivision. It was built more than 12 years ago and has been rock-solid since. We had minor flooding in our neighborhood during the so-called "Tax Day" flood in April 2016. I had noticed some slippage indicated by the foundation expansion joint on the north side of my house then. Yes! I know this is too much information, but it's necessary to set up the ethical dilemma we're going to consider.

Next, came hurricane Harvey flooding where my house was surrounded by water. About two weeks after the flood water had receded, I noticed the expansion joint in my north wall was completely open. Cracks started appearing in my walls, ceiling and in my floor. I believed the water had caused the northeast corner of my foundation to sink because the water had washed away the supporting soil.

I asked my foundation contractor his opinion. He was very noncommittal, citing all kinds of other factors that could be involved. He mentioned that houses built on cul-de-sacs next to man-made lakes frequently had this kind of problem. He did admit that having floodwater surrounding my foundation for days may have been a precipitating factor. But, he certainly wouldn't say that it was the main factor.

Because most houses on my street and within my neighborhood had suffered significant damage from the flood, I asked him about getting FEMA to pay for the damage. I reasoned that my house would simply be lumped in with all the other flooded and damaged houses. Hence, my claim wouldn't be unusual because of the widespread damage in the neighborhood. Again, he was totally noncommittal, providing little support for my rationalizations.

I hope you can see where I was going with this discussion. I had significant damage done to my house. Although I had seen some slippage in my wall joints before the Harvey flood, I was confi-

> So, I was faced with an ethical dilemma. Did I make this claim, knowing in my heart, that I wasn't certain the Harvey flooding caused the damage?

dent that the Harvey flood was the tipping point in causing the damage.

But, I wasn't certain. And, I wasn't going to receive any assistance from my foundation contractor. So, I was faced with an ethical dilemma. Did I make this claim, knowing in my heart, that I wasn't certain the Harvey flooding caused the damage? Or, did I simply assume the attitude that I pay my taxes, everyone else is making FEMA claims, and I should make mine getting my "fair" share of the government money.

> Our ethical comfort zone is established by our Ethical Fence, some call it a "line in the sand." It's an invisible mental line that distinguishes between ethical or unethical actions or divides right from wrong.

Using my "advanced" ethical intelligence, I pondered this question for weeks. I considered all the "facts" of the situation. My house is in the Houston area. An area notoriously known for its shifting soil. My house was built next to a man-made lake, probably setting on dirt excavated from said lake. Floodwater from Harvey surrounded my house, washing away valuable foundation-supporting soil. But, I had seen foundation slippage before Harvey. Fixing the damage was going to cost a ton of money.

I must admit the last "fact" was a very important item. In the end, though, I made a judgment against filing a claim. There wasn't any single factor that brought me to that ethical judgment. I did what any rational engineer-turned-accountant numbers guy would do—I listened to my intuition and gut! Filing the claim would have taken me out of my comfort zone.

Don't Leave Your Comfort Zone. We all know about comfort zones. We hear about them in business, sports and entertainment. Normally, comfort zones are described as limiting, barriers or a place from which we should depart if we want to ever get ahead. Google the term "comfort zone" and you'll get almost 20 million hits. Most of those hits are exhortations to leave your comfort zone. I'll give you opposite advice—**don't ever leave your ethical comfort zone. It only leads to heartache.**

Our ethical comfort zone is established by our Ethical Fence, some call it a "line in the sand." It's an invisible mental line that distinguishes between ethical or unethical actions or divides right from wrong. Some know exactly where that line is, having been established by their Internal Compass. Others tell me that line is faint, so faint that, on occasion, they find themselves on the other side of the line before realizing it. Which side of your line are these apartment dwellers? Here's a story from a Harvey survivor who didn't see Houston's goodness during his family's trek to safety.

> *"We floated for miles out of our neighborhood on a rubber raft. Once we reached streets without standing water, we set the raft to the side, picked up our stuff, and started carrying it. We were headed for the area around Rice University, where I have my office and a lot of friends with high and dry homes.*
>
> *"I was with my wife, a family friend and a German shepherd. We had to pass through an impoverished neighborhood. People were coming out of their apartments. The apartments didn't flood. The people weren't going through anything other than sort of celebrating other people's misery.*
>
> *"I mean they're out partying, having fun, thinking it was really funny. Coming out waving guns at us. Telling us to get out of their neighborhood, and that we didn't belong there. They were telling us that they would loot our neighborhood while we're gone.*

"This was particularly hurtful to me because on weekends I teach. I do workshops on STEM for K-12. I go into all those communities and spend my time on the weekends offering free education workshops and mentorship for the kids in those same neighborhoods. So, for the people in the neighborhoods that I spend my time working to help to come out behaving like that was a real blow.

"That's the part that didn't make the news because it wasn't a Houston strong moment. That's the stuff you didn't hear about. Two days ago [in early March 2018], my neighbor had just gotten all his appliances reinstalled, gotten his TV back, thieves broke into the house and stole everything. Even stole all his contractors' tools. Four more houses on the two blocks around my house, in the past two weeks, people have broken in and stolen all their new appliances."

> "I go into all those communities and spend my time on the weekends offering free education workshops and mentorship for the kids in those same neighborhoods."

Dr. Cesare Wright was relating his family's dreadful experience evacuating from their flooded neighborhood. No! His evacuation story wasn't one of human kindness and respect. It was a story of people whose Internal Compass was pointing in a direction most of us would find worthy of condemnation. But we can't deny or bury reality. As I mentioned at the beginning of this chapter, not all of us share the same worldview, resulting in vastly different true ethical True Norths. Dr. Wright's experience attests to that reality.

Fortunately, stories and experiences like this during hurricane Harvey's flooding were not common. But, they happened. Earlier in the book, I related stories of civilian rescuers receiving gunfire and attempts at forcible thefts of their property. Again, these were not common instances, and represented a small percentage of the hundreds of stories I've heard. We'll return to this issue later in the book. Here's a different kind of Harvey Hero story about a suffering veteran doing the right thing despite the personal cost.

Walking Away

"A group from my church was mucking out flooded houses. My manual labor skills were such that I was designated the "utility" person, meaning I ran errands and did other things not requiring me to handle tools. I was tasked with going to the nearest convenience store to get drinks and snacks. I knew exactly where to go, Sam's American Store. I go there all the time to buy gasoline and snacks. It's a little out of the way. But, I know Ralph, the guy who's on duty during the day.

"Ralph's a military veteran who was severely injured in Afghanistan. He has a prosthetic leg and was burned in an explosion. He tries to cover his body as much as possible, but he's not able to cover the injuries to his face. He's grateful to have a job, and it's a joy to know a man who has so risen above his adversities in life. I'd drive an extra ten miles to fill my car just to benefit Ralph.

"It was hard getting to the store that day because the rain had just stopped and the waters were slowly receding. But, the store was busy because the nearby supermarket was still closed. I walked into the store, and it was wall-to-wall customers. I finally worked my way back to the drink cooler, which was next to the stacked cases of bottled water.

"Once I looked at the prices, I knew what the commotion

throughout the store was about. The store owner had steeply increased the prices on almost everything. Bottles of Gatorade that were normally less than $2 a bottle was now $9 a bottle. Twenty-four-bottle cases of water that normally sold for about $4 a case was now $40 a case. One bottle of cold water that was normally about $1.50 was now $5.

"I was shocked! I've been going to that little store for years, and I'd never seen anything like it. I worked my way back up to the front of the store so that I could talk to Ralph. When Ralph glanced at me, out of the corner of his eye, I could see he didn't want to have a conversation. It wasn't hard for him to avoid me, because he was engaged in heated dialogs with his customers complaining about the outrageous prices. But, they were desperate. So, they paid the prices and left.

"After about 25 minutes, business finally slowed down a little. I walked up to Ralph and asked him how long this had been going on. He said, it started two days ago when the store owner came in and raised all the prices. The owner said. 'We weren't going to get any deliveries for about a week. So, we should make as much money from the inventory we had before we had to close the store and wait for more deliveries.'

"Ralph continued, 'I tried to tell him that I didn't think it was right to charge these high prices to people who desperately needed what we had. He told me not to worry about it and just do my job. When I complained again, he told me if I didn't like the prices I could quit and go home.' At that point, I could see Ralph's eyes getting moist.

"He looked at me and said, 'Do you know how hard it is for me to get a job looking the way I do? People don't want to hire me because they think I'm a freak. I don't make much money here, but it's better than laying around at the house looking useless to my kids. I need this job!'

"I could feel the hurt and see the pain in Ralph's eyes. Here was a burly ex-Marine who courageously served his country reduced to a groveling store clerk working for a man with no ethics. I looked at Ralph and told him that I knew that he knew, in his heart, that what he was doing was wrong. There was a long silence, except for people in the line complaining about how long I was taking.

"Slowly, I could see Ralph's body tightening. He stood up as straight as his damaged frame would allow. He looked me straight in the eye, and said, 'You're right. I quit.' He picked up his cell phone and called the owner of the store and told him that he was quitting, locking the store and leaving."

There's a Kenny Rogers song with the lyrics, "You've got to know when to hold 'em, Know when to fold 'em, Know when to walk away ..." As Elizabeth so eloquently related in this story about Ralph, there are times in all our lives when we have to walk away. Sometimes the walking away is easy. On a business trip, for example, we're tempted to pad our expense account. We could come up with a lot of good reasons and documentation for a little extra. We could easily get away with it, but it makes us uncomfortable. It takes us out of our comfort zone. So, we don't. We walk away.

Other times, as in Ralph's case, it's gut-wrenching. Here we have a man, as far as we know, whose physical injuries were healed. The doctors and nurses had healed Ralph's body, but **his spirit was still bleeding.** His job was like a tourniquet, stemming the flow until enough time could pass for real healing to occur. Yet, he had the courage to release the tourniquet and not cross the "line in the sand," his ethical fence. Ralph knew exactly where that fence was, and he stayed within his comfort zone. He walked away.

We all grew up somewhere on earth. The way we view the world is a product of the environment and the place in which we grew up. That worldview informs the workings of our Internal Compass. Our Internal Compass is how we know right from wrong and the position of our Ethical Fence. Our Ethical Fence establishes the boundaries of our comfort zone. Anything that forces you out of your comfort zone should cause you to walk away. I end this chapter with a couple of questions.

Ralph walked away even though the cost was enormous. Would you have had the courage to walk away? Will you have the courage to walk away when your time comes?

> Ralph walked away even though it cost him great pain. Would you have had the courage to walk away? Will you have the courage to walk away when your time comes?

We now turn our attention to emotions. My research has shown that ethical judging is drenched in emotions. Many of us run away from our emotions or allow them to control our lives. I'm going to encourage you to embrace, take charge and use your emotions to lift you to a whole new level of life.

CHAPTER 7
IT'S OKAY TO CRY

Rescued Couple Giving Each Other Solace

We Can Get Through This, Too **Losing a Family Legacy—Liddy's Story.**

"I've lived in this house for 63 years. Wayne and I bought this property for $25,000, two years after we got married. We raised all four of our children here. I've taken care of my grandchildren here. We had Wayne's after-funeral lunch here. We hosted bible-study groups in this room. Wayne and I never saved much preferring to spend money on our family instead. This home was our retirement account and a legacy for our family. Before the flood, it was appraised at $763,000. Now, I don't know what it's worth, if anything.

"I didn't have flood insurance. This is the first time we've ever had water in the house. It got up to five feet deep. FEMA gave me a small grant, but I can't even start rebuilding because the authorities are revising the floodplain building regulations for this neighborhood. So, I come here every day, putter around and weep.

"My children came over and gutted the house for me. Every memory that was in this place ended up out on the curb. I'm glad the city finally came by and picked it all up because it was an awful reminder of everything I've lost. I'm sorry I'm crying like this, but this is so very hard for me to accept. I've cried every day since it happened.

"My children and church family have been a great help, but I feel like a burden. One day, I was independent with resources. A few days later, I had nothing left. And worse, I'm dependent on others. This isn't the way it's supposed to work out. I'll be 86 in a few months. But, I'm starting over. I'm back where I was at age 18, but without the energy and zest for life I had back then.

"Wayne and I lived a good life, a proper life. We raised our children to become good citizens. We went to church. We gave to the poor. And, we helped others whenever we could. Now, he's gone, and I'm left here with fading memories, tears and an overriding fear of what's coming next."

It's Christmas time 2017. Liddy is tearfully telling her story. She's sitting on a folding chair in, what once was, her family room.

CHAPTER 7: IT'S OKAY TO CRY

Gutted Home Flooded By Harvey

Throughout the empty house, there are no walls, only 2 x 4 studs. A faint smell of cleaning solution is still in the air. The bare concrete floor is pristine. Liddy sweeps it every day and mops it once a week. Old habits are hard to break. Besides, it makes this heavily damaged structure still seem like home.

From the outside, it still looks like the beautiful home it once was. The water line stains on the exterior walls are barely perceptible. The debris is gone, and the yard looks like any other yard during a Houston winter. The towering majestic oak trees that line the streets of this neighborhood show no outward signs of the catastrophic flooding that inundated everything just four months ago.

This is a place frozen in time. People's lives are in limbo. Some have simply sold out for pennies on the dollar and walked away. Others are determined to reclaim their legacy and rebuild. Most, like Liddy, are waiting, living in apartments, hotels or with family. Each of the homes in this once-upscale Houston neighborhood host a family life story, some more than one. Most are like Liddy's, but some are different, reflecting the diversity of people living there. The one common element all these lives share is a mosaic of emotions, an ancient unseen partner.

Embracing an Ancient Partner

Humans have an uncomfortable relationship with emotions, some might call it a love-hate relationship. Most of us enjoy laughter because it feels good, and, now science has demonstrated, that laughing is physically good for our body. Most of us love being in love because there are few other wondrous states of life that compare. Many of us try to avoid anger because negative outcomes can follow anger. In this chapter we're going to look at these apparent contradictions using our hurricane Harvey flooding experiences as a metaphorical examining table. As we proceed with our examination, keep this truth in mind—**ethically intelligent people are also emotionally intelligent.**

My emotional experiences since hurricane Harvey have run the gamut from very deep sorrow to great joy, with the sorrow category exceeding joy simply because of my work on this book. My personal hurricane Harvey experience ended joyfully because my house didn't flood but was preceded by fear and dread waiting for the water to stop rising. Then, I began interviewing people for this book.

As soon as the water receded away from my home and enabled me to leave the neighborhood, I headed to downtown Houston and George Brown Convention Center. I previously related my experience at the convention center. It was nearly a crushing place of sorrow because of the losses suffered by the people I interviewed. They cried, and I cried with them.

Driving from downtown Houston back to my home in Cypress, was long and tedious, made that way by the bumper-to-bumper traffic caused by still-flooded roads. That slow drive offered an opportunity for thought and contemplation. I knew that I wanted to vicariously experience what the survivors and rescuers experienced so that their emotional gestalt would make it into this book.

I wanted to accurately capture the moment so that when you read these pages you would feel what they felt. It was an important part of my mission bringing you an accurate portrayal of the whole of the Harvey flooding experience. I hope I've succeeded. My approach, however, has had a downside.

When I arrived back home that day, Linda looked at me and said, "What happened to you?" I told her that I had just had four-to-five hours of some of the most gut-wrenching experiences ever in listening to survivors tell me about their rescues and losses. I had been weeping in the car on the way home. And, I guess I looked like an emotional wreck.

She looked at me a little more closely and said, "You're not going to anymore rescue centers! You've become too much of an empath to expose yourself to anymore of that kind of sorrow!" As much as I wanted to visit the NRG rescue center the next day, I knew she was right. I had enough "rescue center" material for my purposes.

> It's okay to cry. It's okay to feel. It's okay to identify with the emotions of others. It's one of the amazing gifts of being human. ... it produced a **flood of human goodness.**

I share this with you to make a point. It's okay to cry. It's okay to feel. It's okay to identify with the emotions of others. It's one of the amazing gifts of being human. It's also one of the wonderful things that happened during hurricane Harvey in Houston. And, it produced a **flood of human goodness.**

Now, let's consider some of the emotional experiences of others. Harris County Judge Ed Emmett is the CEO of the third largest county in the country and Director of Homeland Security and Emergency Management for Harris county. He offered this experience.

> "I was in our Office of Emergency Management for six nights. I Got 11 hours of sleep during all that time. I fielded a lot of calls about this issue or that issue and made lots of decisions.
>
> "When I finally left the OEM, and maybe a day or two after it was over, I went to visit my daughter who lives in Braes Heights. That whole neighborhood had flooded, her family was taken out by boat. Fortunately, her home didn't flood. So, she was giving away shoes in her front yard. She and South Main Baptist church were giving away hundreds, thousands of pairs of shoes.
>
> "I drove over there to help. I turned on her street and saw all the debris piled on both sides of the street. I was talking to our legislation relations director at the county and I said, Donna, I've got to pull over. I've got to have a minute. I just basically lost it at that point. Because you see whole lives out on the curb. So, that was probably my darkest hour. Again, it was after the fact. That's the good news."

Judge Ed Emmett was reflecting on one of the first things he did after ending his forced isolation in the Harris County Office of Emergency Management for the duration of the hurricane Harvey event. We also have Harvey Brain moments, like this one from KTRH's News Anchor and Reporter, Nikki Courtney.

> "We were on the air a few days after the World Series. And, somebody called into the newsroom in the middle of the World Series Parade to report that the trains were backed up and that you couldn't get downtown using the train. I was taking his information and interviewing him, and he stopped and said,
>
> "'Is this Nikki Courtney?' I said, 'Yes.' He said, 'Oh my God', I was listening to you during Harvey! He started telling me the story. And, I broke down sobbing. There was another woman who called shortly after Harvey. And, I guess for me, what touched me most, now that I'm thinking back and reliving it ... I mean, I was in the control room talking to people who were listening and that it worked! Here I was sitting in a room talking to myself desperately hoping that I could make a difference in somebody's life—that I could help—brought tears of gratitude to my eyes"

Our Limbic System. Welcome to one of the most ancient portions of our brain—the limbic system. The limbic system of our brain is not only one of the most primitive but most important. It's the seat of our emotions and where judgments are formed. The limbic system is highly interconnected to other segments of our brain including, and most notably, the nucleus accumbens, the brain's pleasure center.

Even though connected to the prefrontal cortex, the center of rational thought, the limbic system is not involved in "rational thought." Instead the limbic brain is *pure feeling*. Although responsible for learning and long-term memory, the limbic system doesn't "think"—it only feels and is in control of the endocrine system (our hormones—remember the term "raging hormones"), autonomous nervous system, and our sense of smell, which is why smells are so important to memory recreation.

Okay! That's as technical as were going to get in this discussion! Why is this important? And, what does it have to do with Houston's response to hurricane Harvey or ethical intelligence, for that matter? I am going to show you how we were not only drenched in water during hurricane Harvey but also emotions. Now, let's look at some drenching. We start with Chief Acevedo.

Drenched in Water and Emotions

"I got word sometime Sunday [August 27th] that Sergeant Steve Perez was missing. I had seen Steve at the union hall. I have an organization of around 6,500 people, and I had only been here nine months when Harvey arrived. I already knew Steve. He stood out for all the right reasons.

"His wife hadn't heard from him since he left home at 4:00 AM Sunday morning. When I heard that, because I knew his character, I knew in my heart of hearts we were going to have a tragic ending. Our investigators went to work. On Monday night [August 28th] we were at Beltway 8 and the Hardy toll road. We had pinpointed where we thought he was. It was in a 16½ foot underpass."

This commentary from Chief Acevedo came in response to me asking him to describe his darkest moment during hurricane Harvey. He continued his answer.

"My darkest moment was when I knew he was in the water in the underpass. It was still raining. There were TXDOT pumps running, but they couldn't keep up with the rain. It was still flooded to 10 feet deep. And that night we had to decide. My dive team had not slept in more than 36 hours. They hadn't stopped working. All they had eaten were power bars during that 36 hours. I could see the exhaustion in their faces.

"We had to make a decision. We couldn't risk more lives for what we knew, in our hearts, was going to be a recovery, not a rescue. Having to make the decision to leave our Sergeant in there in full uniform in that muddy dirty polluted water ... it bothers me to this day, but you can't risk life for recovery. You just can't.

"The next day I got the call that we found him. Once it sunk in that we lost him. It was hard. When I talked to his wife the previous night, I didn't want to give her false hope. Even though I knew it was highly probable he was trapped in the water. You still hold on to a little bit of hope that maybe he's in a hospital somewhere. That was my darkest moment. As the leader, you're responsible for your men and women ...."

Death of a Public Servant. Chief Acevedo, was describing his darkest moment during hurricane Harvey. I still vividly remember the Chief's press conference on Tuesday afternoon the 29th. It was a very emotional moment for him and for those of us watching or listening. As he recounted that story to me in his office nearly four months later, the emotions were still palpable.

Sheriff Gonzalez related another tragic ending.

> "The recovery operation was a combined effort between us [Harris County Sheriff's Office] and the Houston Police Department, when we found the van and pulled it out of the water. "My team members were out there when the incident first happened. And, we were able to rescue one adult family member. The van had already submerged in the fast-moving water. The water was probably flowing seven knots at the time. And, the van was at least four feet under water—it was already out of sight being carried downstream.
>
> "One family member was able to get out of the van and was holding onto a branch. He was yelling for help, and my team happened to be within earshot of him. He was clinging to a tree branch. We were able to get him out by throwing a lasso to him. He was able to hold onto the rope, and the team pulled him to safety."

The incident Sheriff Gonzalez was describing hit our entire community hard. A white van containing an entire family was swept away by raging flood waters. As the Sheriff described, only one of the seven people in the van escaped as the van went under the water. As the water receded, authorities found the van. The Sheriff continued.

> "We subsequently found the van after the water receded. Four of the six members of the family trapped in the van were children. It's one thing to feel the loss of one person, one is too many, you almost take on the pain of the loss. I

had been a homicide detective for many years and had been in similar moments. I've seen loss of life like that before. But, in this case, it all piled up in one incident—one event. The loss of four children ...

"Afterwards you're on to the next case. It was early in the morning that we discovered the bodies and finished the recovery. We gave updates to the media and talked to the family. Then we moved on to the next case. I know that sounds cold. But, it's just what we have to do.

"The whole thing almost seemed like a war. You finish one battle and then go on to the next. One thing we couldn't do was just put our heads down and give up."

Loss of Four Children. Harris County Sheriff, Ed Gonzalez, was describing his, and his team's, reaction to recovering a family from their van that had been swept into the floodwaters during some of the worst moments of hurricane Harvey flooding. Sheriff Gonzales is a well-seasoned law-enforcement professional who's seen his share of death and destruction. During our conversation, he was visibly moved by this incident.

Now, we consider a different kind of death, that of an arts company. Director Perryn Leech described his reactions to discovering the damage to his theater.

"It was that first journey into the Wortham [Theater] when I just said, 'Okay, this is much, much more serious than we could ever have imagined, and, therefore, as an organization, we need to start planning for life without this theater.' It is a purpose-built theater that is the only one in the city of Houston that can, in any way, host an opera company at its normal scale and its normal side of things. I guess it was that moment...

Flooded Wortham Theater Stairwell

"*The first time I opened the door down to the costume shop and I saw water on the stairs (see nearby photo), knowing it was 15 feet below to the costume shop, that was the moment when I knew, yeah, we're not gonna be here. At that point I* didn't necessarily think this season. There was very minimal water on stage so I always assumed that we would be able to get the stage back up and running quickly.

"At that point I probably hadn't realized all the services, mechanical, electrical and air conditioning were all coming from the basement. I hadn't realized that the whole building would be on life support."

> "The first time I opened the door down to the costume shop and I saw water on the stairs, knowing it was 15 feet below to the costume shop, that was the moment when I knew, yeah, we're not gonna be here."

Near Death of a Theater. Director Leech was recounting his first after-storm visit to the place where his opera company performs its magic. Despite the emotional impact of the moment, Director Leech prepared himself for the daunting task of ensuring the 2017-18 season wasn't lost. As you will learn later in this book, he accomplished his task in spectacular style. We briefly return to KTRH.

> "Cliff Saunders, who does news on the Morning Show, was updating us hourly. He came in with the news that the white van that had been swept away by flood waters with four children inside had been found. There were no survivors. Cliff came in and did the story. He closed the mic. We went to a commercial break.
>
> "Cliff put his head down on the table and just broke down. I remember ripping off my headphones and racing around the room, grabbing him and holding him so tight. I wanted to be that person ... that person who said ... we'll do this. People will die, but we will do this!"

Grief at the Death of Four Children. Nikki Courtney, KTRH NewsRadio Anchor and Reporter, was describing a specific emotional moment that occurred during on air storm coverage of hurricane Harvey. We are not emotional islands. We feel what others feel. We're built that way on purpose.

These four episodes are examples of the continuous dousing of water and emotions during hurricane Harvey and its watery aftermath. Each vignette featured different people from different backgrounds and life experiences reacting to tragedies in normal human ways. All of us don't react the same, but all of us, nonetheless, receive the same occasional emotional shower. In the case of the hurricane Harvey, it was continuous.

How we handle these emotional storms not only affects our personal and professional success in life but also our happiness. Our emotions are our life's silent partner until they're not—silent any longer. Ethically intelligent people understand this truth and strive to train and control their emotional muscles as effectively as they do the muscles that move their arms and legs. Here's an ethically intelligent response, courtesy of Harris County Sheriff Gonzales.

> "We were able to talk to a group from New York. They were organized post-911. They reached out and were very helpful. I have learned that in law enforcement it's necessary to debrief [decompress] after any critical incident. I had been a hostage negotiator and seen loss of life. When I was a homicide detective we never debriefed after an incident.
>
> "After a time, you realize that you are impacted. Even if you dealt with it, there's still an impact. It's an internal one. You can physically bruise, and you feel it. But an internal bruise you don't always see it. So, we went through the prac-

tice of having debriefs. I was involved with the first one. That kind of set the tone. We're grown men ... women...

"I know there's a mask that sometimes we put on in this profession that says, I'm strong. I can handle all that. That's why I put on the badge every day. But it's okay to also say we're human and **we're normal, but we see abnormal things***. And it's okay to talk about these experiences. And some officers opened up. It was a safe zone where we could say whatever we wanted.*

"Look it's really hard. I'm thinking about my daughter when I'm protecting others, but I'm wondering if my own daughter is okay and might need me. Or is my family still at home? Are they safe? So, it was good to let those pressures out because people do internalize them. We want to remember Harvey, but we don't want to keep reliving it. That's the key. We should always remember and learn from but not keep reliving it in our minds."

> "I know there's a mask that sometimes we put on in this profession that says, I'm strong. I can handle all that. That's why I put on the badge every day. But it's okay to also say we're human and **we're normal, but we see abnormal things.**"

Learning to Decompress. Sheriff Gonzalez is on the right track. He instinctively knows that ethically intelligent people are also emotionally intelligent. If you only take away one nugget of wisdom from this book, it's this—humans are a package of physical, mental, spiritual, rational and emotional processes. You can't neglect one item in the package and expect the others will remain untouched and thriving.

Why is this important? It's important because I want you to understand your prefrontal cortex, *your rational mind, is not the engine of your mental life.* It's merely a brake on the real engine—the limbic brain—the feeling you! The great Western philosopher Hume said, "In the face of passion, reason is impotent."

ENGINE OF LIFE

Your limbic brain is the engine of your life. It's your center of motivation. It may "consult" with other parts of the brain, but it makes the final judgment—without thinking—it only feels. Your limbic brain is also the way you connect with other people. Daniel Goleman, author of the book *Emotional Intelligence,* and other researchers coined the term "limbic lock" to describe an unseen process where my limbic system connects with your limbic system.

Goleman used the metaphor of two modems syncing up as a way of describing this function (Yes, I know. No one uses those kinds of modems anymore. But, the analogy fits.). The easiest way for this "syncing up" process to occur is through laughter, which may explain why many speakers start out with a joke. It helps them connect with the audience.

I've validated this theory many times in practice. In speaking to an audience, if I can get them laughing with me, I can sense the connection and subsequent engagement. This is also a technique that I've used successfully in my teaching. If I can get a classroom of students laughing together on the first night of class, the emotional togetherness of the group throughout the remainder of the course is remarkable. Emotion, especially laughter, helps people connect.

> **... your rational mind, is not the engine of your mental life.** It's merely a brake on the real engine—the limbic brain—the feeling you! The great Western philosopher Hume said, "In the face of passion, reason is impotent."

And, connect we did! The connecting emotion was most likely not laughter, although it could've been. I would nominate fear, gratitude and sorrow. Most of us felt some level of fear throughout the event, especially those whose personal safety was threatened. Most of us were grateful for either escaping or being rescued from danger. I believe sorrow was pervasive throughout the event. It was, at least in my case, the strongest emotion because of an overwhelming sense of loss.

There were overwhelming losses during the storm. A large portion of that loss was physical—homes, offices, bridges, roads, cars and furniture. We can quantify those losses in numbers of items and dollars. The losses that are nearly impossible to quantify are intangible and, perhaps, invisible. These might include your sense of financial security, a job, career, business, a sense of self-worth that comes from an ability to provide for yourself and your family, personal or professional success and memories.

> We all became more sensitive and empathic, and it spurred us into action. We volunteered to help one another in such numbers, rescue centers were turning volunteers away.

Regardless of who we are, all of us can identify with these losses and empathize with those who were suffering. Although we may have never personally suffered floodwaters entering our home, we can imagine the pain we would feel watching our home being overrun by flood water. It's also easy for us to imagine the fear and embarrassment that would ensue from losing your income source and not being able to care for your family.

Returning to Goleman's colorful term, we experienced one gigantic "limbic lock" during hurricane Harvey as it ravaged the Houston area. We all became more sensitive and empathic, and it spurred us into action. We volunteered to help one another in such numbers, rescue centers were turning volunteers away. Many of us jettisoned our normal concern about our personal safety and plunged into floodwaters to rescue our neighbors. Our ancient "silent partner" helped us to act quickly and humanely. Here's an example from a civilian rescuer.

> ***"The thought process wasn't really very extensive.*** *It was just something that I was able to do. Then, it was just a matter of finding where I could go to get started. I saw a group of folks gathered up by a house. So, I stopped in and checked out what was going on. That's where I learned about the search and rescue operation.*
>
> *"So, bright and early the next morning I packed a change of clothes, supplies, snacks and everything else I might need because I knew it'd be a long day. I went back to the house from the night before. They assembled us into teams and explained what was going on and what we were going to be doing. The group had already been doing it.*
>
> *"So, I teamed up with a guy and his dog. Besides his dog, he also had a boat. The folks in charge added three more people to our boat. We had me, the guy who owned the boat, his dog and three former U. S. Marines. All the Marines were all from out of town, two guys from East Texas and a woman from Austin. We headed out. I felt safe with that team. We were all packin'.*
>
> *"There's an app that we used that kept us in contact with dispatchers who were working directly with The National*

Guard, the Lieutenant Governor, the Sheriff's office, and others. The group was authorized and cleared. They deputized us and sent us out to look for people. We were to get them to safety, and then evacuate them. Then, dispatch would move us to the next location."

I bolded the first few words of that civilian rescuer's account to make the point. Our limbic brain doesn't "think." It moves us to action. This is why a parent will run back into a burning house to save a child, or even a family pet. Or, why just recently, a total stranger jumped out of their car at the scene of a bridge collapse in Florida. At great peril to her physical safety, the stranger crawled under the teetering bridge and pulled an injured victim from a crushed vehicle.

Please don't get the impression that I'm advocating that we simply let our emotions run rampant in our lives. I am not. But, the emotional component of our humanity is what drives us forward. Emotions make life worth living. Emotions coupled with knowledge become controlled passion. Controlled passion gives us purpose. Controlled passion has given us cures for diseases, technological advances and compassion for one another. It's what gets us out of bed in the morning.

Four days before Christmas 1968, three astronauts were aboard the Apollo 8 spacecraft waiting blastoff. Their mission was to make humanity's first trip to the moon and back. Lunar module pilot, Major William Anders recalled, "Sitting on top of the Saturn V, which was a mini nuclear bomb itself."

Major Anders and his colleagues weren't sitting atop a mini nuclear bomb just because their rational minds decided it was a logically sound thing to do. Yes, they were certainly rational men, each one a scientist and engineer. Despite that rationality, they were sitting in that precarious position, where they couldn't even see outside the capsule, because their passion for space flight and exploration drove them forward.

Learn to love your emotions. They're your friends. You can run, but you can't hide from them. Embrace the entire you! Learn the art of controlled release of this powerful aspect of your humanity. See the goodness it brings to your life. **We saw the goodness it produced during hurricane Harvey in Houston.**

Lest you think this ethically intelligent Houston behavior is new and only flowered during hurricane Harvey, I'll leave you with this story from 2005, as told by Former Harris County Judge Robert Eckels. It shows that Houston has been full of goodness for a long time.

> "People think Katrina was a disaster for the people of New Orleans. It was, but it was a disaster here too. We had a quarter million people come to Houston from New Orleans. It was a shelter operation. Houstonians here were similarly good. I remember people from New Orleans telling me they pulled up to a gas station and somebody would see their Louisiana license plates and buy their gas.
>
> "We housed thousands of them in the Astrodome. There was a cultural difference between the folks from New Orleans and Houston. There was a much stronger racial divide and much bigger class divide in New Orleans compared to Houston. And I distinctly remember this women, who was wearing a silk blouse and matching slacks. She was from the Woodlands, a well-dressed volunteer.
>
> We had 60,000 volunteers working and here she was carrying a tray of drinks around to people from New Orleans's lower 9th ward. These folks were largely black, low income,

some of the most impoverished of the poor people from New Orleans. Here she was serving drinks as these rescuees came and sat around the tables.

What was telling about it was not so much that they were getting drinks but that here you had this woman that had probably never interacted with folks of this social status before, and these folks were just amazed that there was a rich white woman from the Woodlands passing out drinks to them. This guy came up to me later and said, 'I used to hate white people.' And, I said we don't care about that here in Houston."

> "... folks were just amazed that there was a rich white woman from the Woodlands passing out drinks to them. This guy came up to me later and said, 'I used to hate white people.' And it was like, we don't care about that here in Houston."

Judge Eckels was reflecting on the similarities between Houston's response to hurricanes Katrina and Harvey. His point was, this community hasn't changed over the 13 years since hurricane Katrina in 2005. We welcomed almost 250,000 refugees from the New Orleans area in 2005, and we displayed the same goodness that was on display during hurricane Harvey, except on a much smaller scale in the case of hurricane Katrina.

In this chapter, we've talked about learning to love your emotions all over again. In our current culture, emotions get an undeserved bad rap. Many of us take great pride in living a no-drama life. We place our rational minds on pedestals, lift our noses a bit higher into the air and proclaim— "Emotions don't rule me!" Wanna bet? Ethically intelligent people know emotions are the engine of life. We also know how to harness the engine's energy to live life to the fullest. You can too!

Remember, ethically intelligent people are also emotionally intelligent.

Now, we move on to experiencing what leading from the eye of the storm looks like.

CHAPTER 8

LEADING FROM THE EYE OF THE STORM

Leadership News Conference During Hurricane Harvey

"A political leader's career is made or broken during disasters, whether it's a big rain or flood here, a snow storm in Baltimore or something else in New York City. When there's a crisis, people want to see that government works, responding to that crisis. Most people don't really care about the difference between rural, city, state or the federal government. To them it's all government. They just want it to work. So, you need to be wearing your big leader britches and not be blaming the city, the county or someone else for problems. A leadership partnership showing everyone working together and working through whatever issues you've got is what people expect."

Former Harris County Judge Robert Eckels was sharing his views on the requirements and hazards of public emergency leadership. He went on to say that no matter what kinds of differences there are among the leadership team, behind the scenes, a united public presentation is a necessity for success. I believe we had such a team, as pictured above, during hurricane Harvey and its aftermath.

As a leadership professor and expert, I give this team an A+ for their hurricane Harvey leadership. Were there problems? Yes, there always are. Was the planning perfect? No, it rarely is. Were some parts of the Houston Metropolitan Area underserved? Yes, hopefully that will be addressed. Was there enough rescue equipment? No, not even close to filling the need. Crowdsourced equipment, however, partially filled the void.

Despite these apparent shortcomings, our public and private leadership poured their hearts and souls into serving the people of this metropolitan area, and they did it with distinction. As this chapter unfolds, you'll see why I mention *apparent* shortcomings. No one can adequately plan for an event that is magnitudes larger than any previous similar event. Remember, Harvey's rains were a once-in-a-42,000-year-rain event! And, I don't think anyone would like the taxes necessary to keep thousands of boats and high-water vehicles in storage waiting for the next event!

As you read this chapter, you'll learn a lot you may not know about our leaders. I did. And, I was impressed. All of them graciously accepted my invitation to participate in interviews that were close and personal. I think what you'll learn may come as a pleasant surprise. Everyone you'll hear from in this chapter is a servant leader, only one step below the best type of leadership, which is the gardener leader. I'll discuss that type of leader later in the chapter. Now, let's consider casualties.

The First Two Casualties Are...

Many believe the first two casualties of war are truth and the plan, in that order. Was hurricane Harvey a war? Maybe, not in the sense that people were shooting at one another ... well, there were reports ... I digress. Bombs weren't dropping ... well, there was that one big explosion ... I digress again. Buildings weren't blown apart ... well, there were some tornadoes and roofs blown away. Many of the first responders I interviewed said it seemed like war. I think you get my drift.

First, we'll consider truth. Except for the disputed communications swirling around the dam releases we discuss in the next chapter, we heard the "truth" from our leaders during the hurricane Harvey emergency. I placed the word truth in quotation marks because, believe it or not, we don't always agree on what the truth is. I've written about this subject earlier in this book and elsewhere. So, I won't do a deep dive into the matter here.

Suffice it to say, truthfulness may be an elusive concept to some of us. To ensure that we're all on the same page, I'm going to repeat my definition of truthfulness. This definition governs my conclusions about truth telling during the hurricane Harvey emergency. Truthfulness is, **telling or having the intention of telling the truth, which is defined as accurately and sincerely describing reality (including the context of that reality), as known by the person describing that reality.**

In other words, when you relate your "facts," do you sincerely believe those "facts" are correct given the relevant context involved? During most emergencies, "facts" are hard to come by. The hurricane Harvey emergency was no different. But, the proliferation of "facts" was made more difficult by social media. Okay. I can see the eyes rolling. I realize that most of us got a lot of our hurricane Harvey information from social media. As the rain drenched us with water, social media drenched us with information. Unfortunately, some of that information was outright wrong or, lacking enough context for it to be useful.

Bryan Erickson, director of AM radio operations for iHeart Media in Houston made that point, "There was a constant stream of info coming in on Twitter and Facebook and, as we've all discovered, it's not always easy to separate fact from fiction." Most of the civilian rescuers I interviewed, also reporting using social media extensively. They reported that a lot of the information they received, even from "official" dispatchers was wrong, which poses the interesting question—"Were those dispatchers lying?"

Most of us would answer that question in the negative. The dispatchers were passing on information they believed was correct. As it turned out, some of it was wrong. Did it waste a lot of time and resources? Yes. Could it have been avoided? Probably not. During an emergency, everyone is hungry, even desperate, for information. Most of us pass on what we think we "know" without any verification or hesitation. And, in most cases, verification wasn't possible anyway.

Here's a real-time professional example from Nikki Courtney trying to sort out facts from fiction under adverse circumstances.

> *"You kind of do what you have to do. ... During the storm coverage, the hardest thing was trying to harness and evaluate all the information, like Twitter. I'd see something and think,*

CHAPTER 8: LEADING FROM THE EYE OF THE STORM

THAT'S important, but then I'd go through another 20 tweets and think, THAT's important.

"How do you isolate the important ... the good information? We had a TV. We had computers. Something would be on TV... and I would think, THAT'S important. But, when the mic was open, the information wasn't still in front of me.

"I found the most valuable tool I had was the camera on my phone. I took pictures of tweets. I took pictures of the television. I took pictures of what was on a computer screen. So as you were listening to me, as I was rattling off information, I was going through my phone passing on my informational pictures. For me, that was ... the mother of invention—the necessity of good information."

> ... leaders must tell the truth, first to themselves and then to everyone else. And, they must demand the truth from those they lead.

Nikki was describing her struggle not only with reporting important information but also sifting through potentially suspect information. As news consumers, we're quick to criticize the news media for getting it wrong. In many cases, especially given our polarized politics these days, they rightly deserve the criticism. During hurricane Harvey storm coverage, however, the news media, especially local news media, acquitted themselves with distinction.

I am a leader. I've worked for and observed scores of excellent leaders in action, and I've studied leadership for decades. Out of that accumulated information, knowledge and wisdom I can say two things for certain—leaders must tell the truth, first to themselves and then to everyone else. And, they must demand the truth from those they lead.

Without truth, leadership fails. Hardship and heartache soon follow. We all know the Enron story and its aftermath. Truth is the foundation of ethical intelligence, as we learned in Chapter 3. So, how did our leaders perform during hurricane Harvey and its aftermath?

I'll answer that question by making observations and citing real-world examples. Leadership is break-tested in crises and emergencies. Leading is easy when the sun is shining and all is flowing smoothly. That all changes when your city's underwater, operational plans go down the drain with the rainwater and there are cries for help that you can't answer.

Harris County Sheriff Ed Gonzalez commented on his personal leadership break-test.

> *"I remember the rain starting at night. The next day came, and the rain just wouldn't stop. Then, coming back to headquarters, I could see the jail was coming under severe stress in terms of the systems, our tunnels our walkways. And, at that moment, I was like—I have to keep it together. We have to get through this. We have to navigate this, literally.*
>
> *It wasn't just go out there and rescue. We were operating a jail, with both staff and inmates. We had over 8,000 inmates locked up. We were responsible for their care and custody. Our staff, was now literally on an island where they couldn't leave. Keeping their morale up was a major priority. We made the rounds as much as possible to thank them.*
>
> *Hurricane Harvey and the flooding was a devastating event and caused tremendous losses. But, on the flip side we saw teamwork. We saw great leadership come before us. So, as a native Houstonian, when the rain just wouldn't stop, I remember thinking, my God what is happening to my hometown?*

> *I was just one individual. But, I wanted to make sure that I did everything I could to help protect my hometown and my county. I committed to leading the men and women that serve within the Harris County Sheriff's office to excellence at our city's greatest time of need. It was all hands on deck starting from the Sheriff to the last person.*

Sheriff Gonzalez had been in office only eight months when hurricane Harvey arrived. Saying it was a baptism under fire ... no, under water ... would be an understatement. In his comments, we see the burden of leadership take its toll on a man determined to excel in some of the worst crisis circumstances possible. He rose to the occasion because he leads from the front.

Houston Police Chief Art Acevedo is another leader who leads from the front.

> "I was out there with our men and women leading from the front. ... I love being a leader. I don't mind the burden. Some say there's a burden of leadership, I think it's the privilege of leadership. I focus on the privilege. I volunteered to be here. So, don't wee-wee for me. I'm not going to wee-wee for myself. I tell my men and women, there's a great responsibility when you're a leader. There's a lot of sacrifice that comes with leadership.
>
> "I help my people do their job. As leaders of this organization, we were there in the trenches with our people, which sometimes is not the culture of policing. Sometimes people think oh it's not my job, I've got four stars. That's BS. You lead from the front. You build emotional capital by sacrificing, doing what you ask your people to do. I didn't go home and sleep in my bed even though I could have. I live 3.7 miles from here [police headquarters]. I stayed here with my people.

> "I haven't forgotten where I came from. This country gave us the greatest gift of all as Cuban refugees in 1968. My father said it gave us the gift of freedom. There's no greater gift on earth. My parents used to tell us don't ever forget that the worst day in the United States is better than the best day in the Communist world. Don't ever forget that."

Chief Acevedo was discussing his views on leadership and relating how he applied those views during hurricane Harvey. Chief Acevedo isn't new to leadership. Prior to coming to Houston, he led the police department of Austin, Texas, and before that within the California Highway Patrol. His leadership style is that of a servant leader, which closely lines up with his faith in God.

Harris County Judge Ed Emmett was quick to give credit to his people and organization.

> "I'll be out in public and people will come up and say 'Oh you did such a great job!' And I appreciate that. I'm not trying to be overly modest. The reality is I'm the face of a very professional organization, and they do what they're supposed to do. ... We have a full-time office of emergency management, and we prepare for all types of emergencies. ...
>
> I've got a professional staff. I've been through hurricane Ike. I've been through numerous floods. I've been through ice storms. And, we're just used to it. Once we activate our Emergency Operations Center, everybody just gets to work. I don't want to make it sound light-hearted, but it's just what we do."

CHAPTER 8: LEADING FROM THE EYE OF THE STORM

Judge Ed Emmett is the Chief Executive/Administrative officer and Director of Homeland Security and Emergency Management for Harris County, Texas, the third-largest county, by population, in the country. He leads an organization tasked with providing services to 4.7 million people residing in a county comprising a land mass of 1,778 square miles, almost the size of the state of Delaware.

> "There's no limit to what you can accomplish if you don't care who gets the credit."
>
> This attitude is the mark of a mature and self-confident leader ...

In his succinct comments, Judge Emmett was reflecting a leadership philosophy President Ronald Reagan espoused, **"There's no limit to what you can accomplish if you don't care who gets the credit."** This attitude is the mark of a mature and self-confident leader who's recruited a great leadership team and has confidence in that team to get the job done.

Mayor Sylvester Turner is cut from the same leadership mold as Judge Emmett. He gives his leadership team the credit for his success.

> "Tom McCasland, Houston's Housing and Community Development Department Director, and his team set up and managed the George R. Brown rescue center. And, they did a phenomenal job. It was well organized. And, when you go from expecting a couple of thousand rescuees ... and don't have any time to prepare ... to 10,000 people literally almost overnight, it was incredible. They did a masterful, masterful job. ...

In our interview, Mayor Turner related several stories about his leadership team's performance. I told some of those stories in Chapter 5. All the stories, like this rescue center story, have the same theme—recruit good people and let them do their jobs. In other words, leaders keep their eyes on the big picture.

Bob Harvey, President and CEO of the Greater Houston Partnership, summed it up best.

> *"Our civic leadership—our mayor and our county judge, just to reduce it to the two of them—exemplified our civic leadership. They were acting responsibly, not casting blame or aspersions, working cooperatively, not worrying about rules but doing what needed doing. And, asking the question, 'What's the right thing to do?'*
>
> *"So, you saw it in the leadership. And, then, you saw the community responding. We saw neighbor helping neighbor, stranger helping stranger. I would say the leadership got out into the public quickly. I think that helped motivate, even the individual responses. Maybe, they were unrelated. I can't prove it ... but I think the fact that our leadership was acting responsibly helped support the idea that we all needed to pitch in. It was remarkable."*

> ... our leaders presented a united, collaborative and cooperative example. Our community followed that example. Our leaders acted ethically intelligently.

Bob Harvey's commentary is packed with leadership wisdom we should all internalize. The most important is "tone" begins at the top. Our leaders led by example. People pay more attention to what you do rather than what you say. As CEO Harvey observed, regardless of what may have been occurring behind the scenes, our leaders presented a united, collaborative and cooperative example. Our community followed that example. Our leaders acted ethically intelligently. Our community followed suit and displayed that goodness.

I started this chapter introducing two casualties of war and public emergencies or crises, the first of which was truth. Was truth a casualty during hurricane Harvey and its aftermath? My answer is a resounding NO! Our leaders conveyed the "facts" as they knew them at the time they conveyed those "facts". In retrospect, we might say those "facts" later proved incorrect. That may be true. Hindsight is always 20/20. If there was no intent to deceive, there is no lying.

Telling and hearing the truth is a foundational element of leadership. Our leadership team passed that test with flying colors. Now, we examine the second casualty of war, public emergencies or crises—The Plan. We begin by introducing the guy who is normally behind the scenes when emergency plans are created. His forecasts are one of the cornerstones of any weather-related emergency plan.

Play-By-Play of an Unfolding Disaster

Jeff Lindner, is the Chief Meteorologist of the Harris County Flood Control District. Jeff was on local television so frequently during hurricane Harvey and its flooding, his persona became almost synonymous with the emergency itself. As it turned out, Jeff became our **play-by-play announcer of the unfolding disaster** known as hurricane Harvey.

The most memorable personal image I have of Jeff during those days is one appearance where he had four guys holding two large exhibits during his entire presentation, which lasted at least 20 minutes. I had great admiration for the arm-stamina displayed by those guys during that presentation. But, I digress.

Jeff is an Aggie's Aggie. And, I mean that as a compliment! We met in a large windowless conference room whose walls were covered in maps and video screens. There was also a phone bank. Jeff said this was Ground Zero for them during emergencies. Thankfully, that day it was deadly silent.

I was interested in hearing from Jeff because his planning and subsequent forecasting of storm activity drove much of the organized governmental emergency response. I knew that both the city of Houston and Judge Emmett's organizations relied on information that Jeff's organization was supplying for their planning and subsequent response. So, here's a small portion of what he told me.

Jeff's has a remarkable command of storm facts, historical comparisons, and his encyclopedic knowledge of this area's rainfall, flood plains and watersheds is amazing. His perspective adds an indispensable dimension to the story of hurricane Harvey and Houston. I hope you enjoy reading it as much as I did, hearing and distilling it.

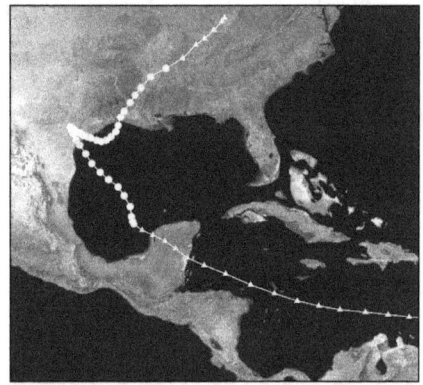

Hurricane Harvey's Path

> "The forecasts, were very good leading up to the storm, and never changed much. Hurricane Harvey was always a mid-Texas coast landfall. The forecast intensity was off a bit. Initially Harvey was forecast to be a Category 1—it ended up being a Category 4 storm. But we see that speed of development, from time to time, in the Gulf of Mexico. You can get storms that develop very quickly like Harvey, whose track appears in the nearby photo.

"After landfall there was always an indication of a slowing, a looping motion, and then moving back up to the Northeast up towards the Houston area. So that possibility was always in the models. Now how exactly that transpired and where the heavy rainfall happened was always kind of the question leading up to something like this."

Mission Critical Information. This is the type of information our leaders needed for making critically informed decisions that impact our community's safety. Both Judge Emmett and Mayor Turner mentioned Jeff's data as crucial in their preparations for the storm. Jeff continued.

"What was unique about Harvey is all the model guidance was on the same page, there was going to be some really big rainfall. And, what I mean by that is we were talking 20, 25, 30, 35 inches of rain, which is a lot of water output for forecast models. There were some models that were even up to 50, 55 inches, which is rare, even unheard of. Never have we seen such totals on the forecast models. Normally, a model outputting 12 or 15 inches of rain is a lot.

"So, when we began seeing those extreme numbers, the first question we asked is, 'Is this really going to happen?' I think we were all, in the back of our heads thinking, Yeah, we see it, yes there's a lot of consistency, but is this really going to happen?

"Historically, what happens is we get those rain totals, but it's going to fall in small areas, like a portion of a county or a portion of a region. Very rarely do we see it, if ever, over such a large area. That was the other factor we were skeptical about, were we really going to see this much rain over such a big area.

"As we got into the Friday night landfall and then Saturday, and the storm started to slow down, began meandering back toward the east, toward us, we started getting into the smaller timescales. It was during the day Saturday that some of these smaller models were starting to show big rains during Saturday night over Harris County."

"The models were very consistent hour after hour showing this so we really had some good confidence on Saturday. Up until Saturday evening, we hadn't seen a whole lot of rain. We had rain, but it wasn't anything that we couldn't handle.

Fast Rising Water

"But we knew, potentially, the situation was set to get really bad Saturday night. We began warning the public on Saturday that, 'We understand the storm's made landfall, we understand up until this point everything has been okay, but don't let your guard down.' And it was Saturday night when conditions got very bad, and quickly."

A Developing Catastrophe. This was a critical turning point in the storm's time over Houston. Mayor Turner, Chief Acevedo and Sheriff Gonzalez mentioned Jeff's forecast and warnings in our conversations. All three noted how important knowing the forecast was in their mobilization of resources. In retrospect, we can see this turning point. At the time, however; it wasn't obvious at all. Our leaders and the public were rightly skeptical of the unprecedented forecasts Jeff and other weather organizations were making. Jeff was skeptical. He expanded on his narration of the developing catastrophe.

"Historically, when we have a flood, for example Tax Day 2016 and Memorial Day 2015, those happened very fast. We went from virtually nothing happening to flooding in 3 or 4 hours. That's how Harvey initially started. We got big rains quickly 4, 5 or 6 inches an hour. It resulted in tremendous amounts of runoff in a short period of time.

"The water comes up in the streets. The water rises in the creeks and bayous. The problem is if it keeps raining, you start to get flooding. The rain overwhelms the drainage system. The creeks and bayous fill. The systems designed to handle the water fill. That happened Saturday night into Sunday. By Sunday morning early, about 2:00 AM, we realized it was going to be bad.

"My statement about really bad is our benchmark flood up to Harvey was tropical storm Allison in 2001. When we began seeing water levels reach and exceed tropical storm Allison levels, which happened around 1:00 to 2:00 AM Sunday, we knew we had a record-setting event. The rains and the rising water, especially in the cities of South Houston and Pasadena and, then, southeast Harris county was something we had never seen.

"About that same time we started getting a lot of 911 calls reporting chest-and-neck-deep water in homes. Calls were coming both into the 911 center and into our phone bank in this room. We had three operators on our phone bank. That's rare for us. It's not very often that we get that deep of water in homes around here because the area is so flat the water can just spread out. It's shallow but over a wide area."

At that moment, Sunday morning, August 27th, a collective epiphany occurred. This storm was unlike any this area had ever experienced, at least since recordkeeping began. Conditions were spiraling into unprecedented, unknown and dangerous territory. Jeff continued his narration.

Unprecedented Water Depths

"In Harvey's case it covered a wide area and was getting very deep. So, between seeing that we were hitting or exceeding Allison levels and getting the calls of severely flooded homes, we knew we were in a situation we had never faced before. We had some of this type of flooding with Allison, where the water got high in some isolated areas. But this time it was different because it was happening over such a large area and at the same time. So, from Pasadena down to South Houston, over to Hobby airport, and, then, it began spreading up to the north.

"As the morning went on, the rains expanded. So, it engulfed the entire county, then, not only the entire county but the entire region. That was really the big difference. If you look at everything we faced in the past, Allison in 2001 and Claudette 1979, which is still the US 24-hour rainfall record of 43 inches, those were point rainfalls in a specific location."

"For example, Claudette 1979 sat right over Alvin in Brazoria county. If you drove north to downtown Houston, however; we only got about 6 or 8 inches of rain. In Allison, you had about 28-30 inches of rain in 12 hours, but it was in one small portion of Harris county just south of Lake Houston.

"Harvey was not to that level of extreme rainfall amounts in a short period of time, but 20-25 inches over a very large area in about a 12-24-hour period. That's just a tremendous *amount of rain over a large area. I think some people neglected the significance of the rainfall because we'd never experienced it before."*

As he continued his description of these moments, I could sense the frustration this man of science felt during the event. Prior records were not only being broken but shattered. Jeff was searching for the words to use in reporting the developing gravity of the emergency to community leadership without losing credibility and creating panic. Jeff resumed his comparisons.

"The amount of rain that Harvey dropped over such a large area is something we've never seen before, ever, in Harris county, in the state of Texas, and even in the nation. The previous worst storm ever that covered 2,000 square miles over a 5-day period, produced about 29.8 inches of rain in the state of Louisiana in 1940. That was the worst storm ever—until Harvey.

"Hurricane Harvey, for that same special coverage—2,000 square miles, five-day period—produced almost 44 inches of rain [53 inches in some areas]. Almost 14 inches more rain than the worst storm we've ever seen in the nation. That's just mindboggling. If you can imagine the worst storm ever, then exceed that by over a foot, you can't mentally process it. Because in dealing with weather, hydrology and rainfall you usually beat records by a tenth of an inch or a hundredth of an inch.

When we talk about water levels rising in channels, bayous and rivers you might normally eke passed the previous limit. In this case, we just blew passed records by feet. Buffalo bayou was five feet over the previous record. Places on Greens

> bayou blew right passed the previous record, four or five feet passed. Even months later, it's still difficult to comprehend the scale of hurricane Harvey."

Jeff's discourse shows how unforeseen reality destroys even the best plans. The pre-Harvey private and public-sector organization emergency and crisis plans were based on the historical data and patterns Jeff mentioned. When those data and patterns changed dramatically, plans became inadequate quickly.

Imagine introducing a new product, and your most optimistic forecast calls for selling one million units during the first year. All your infrastructure is driven by the forecast—supply chain, manufacturing, inventory levels, shipping, distribution and marketing. Then, the product hits the market, and one million units sell in the first month! Many would say, "Wow! That's a great problem to have."

Tell that to a CEO who's faced with livid customers, overwhelmed suppliers, exhausted employees, angry shareholders and empty warehouses. Plus, the CEO is subject to 24/7 public ridicule at the hands of cable business news talking heads! Anybody remember Apple and the iPhone? Just sayin'!

In many ways, that's exactly what happened to Houston Metropolitan Area organizational leadership teams across the spectrum of private/public sectors as hurricane Harvey spread misery across the area. Nonetheless, those teams rose to the occasion. Here are some of their stories, starting with Houston's Police Chief Acevedo placing his department on an emergency footing.

> "I've seen a lot of manmade and natural disasters. I worked and lived through the Northridge earthquake, numerous California mudslides and firestorms, the Los Angeles riots and the

Widespread Harvey Flooding

Gulf war riots in San Francisco. So, I've been through a lot of disasters in my career. I've seen a lot of destruction. including the Rodney King riots, which were the most destructive in American history.

"*But, I've never seen the destruction that I saw during hurricane Harvey. From the news coverage, I don't think people could appreciate how widespread the destruction was here in Houston. Harvey took the soon to be 3rd largest city in the nation, and turned it into a series of islands, as shown in the nearby photo.*

"*A lot of people didn't believe we were gonna get 50+ inches of rain, but I did. I was constantly monitoring 20+ weather apps I have. In one of the first meetings with all my command staff, I told them, 'Folks, what we are about to face is gonna be of Biblical proportions.'*"

Chief Acevedo was reacting to the forecasts Jeff Lindner was just discussing. Unlike many others, including me, Chief Acevedo believed the forecasts he was seeing. Having been unprepared in the past, he wasn't about to let that happen again. We continue with Chief Acevedo's description.

> "I went through what were called the Halloween floods in Austin. We were not well prepared, and we didn't respond well. I'm a guy that doesn't make the same mistake twice, generally. I think you must have an operational mindset when you're facing something of a magnitude that ... that's never been faced before.
>
> "So, one of the things I told my people was, 'Forget what we've learned in past storms. Forget how we responded in past storms, because what we're about to experience has never been experienced.' I'm not making that up. You can talk to any of my team, and they'll tell you. I wanted to make sure people understood what can hurt an organization is being surprised, when you underestimate what's about to happen, as shown in the nearby photo of rooftop flooding.
>
> "I wanted my people to have the right frame of mind. I told everybody in this organization, 'One, make sure your families are prepared because you're not going to be there for them. We're going to be working. Two, something of Biblical proportions is coming. Three, be prepared, no one's going home. We're going to hold you hostage.'
>
> I wanted to establish an operational rhythm early and identify any challenges. A lot of organizations wait until the storm hits to go on tactical alert. We started 24 hours early at 6:00 PM on Friday, even though we weren't anticipating

'Forget what we've learned in past storms. Forget how we responded in past storms, because what we're about to experience has never been experienced.'

the heavy rain starting until Saturday night. Then, I put the entire department on 24-hour shifts starting the second day of the storm."

Chief Acevedo was describing his process for converting a static lifeless emergency plan into an operational reality. He was also demonstrating shifting from his normal leadership style into a situational leadership style, a process leadership guru John Maxwell described as, "Read the need, then lead." Effective leaders understand that a single leadership style is not appropriate under all circumstances. Now, let's have a look at the private sector.

Previously Unseen Rooftop Flooding

Cindy Yeilding is Senior Vice President of BP America, which is headquartered in Houston. BP's story is both revealing and heartwarming. We'll revisit BP and Cindy in Chapter 10. Here, she describes putting their plan into action.

"From a preparation perspective, we were actually quite fortunate. We were having a BP America Board of Directors

meeting, which meant that all the leaders from around the United States were together in one room or available on the phone. On Thursday the 24th, we began monitoring the weather forecasts. After it became apparent the storm was going to hit Texas, we activated our emergency response.

"So, what does that mean? There are certain parts of our business that must stay operational 24-hours a day, so the magnitude of the storm triggered a move that Thursday before the storm. Several of our operations, probably the biggest one being our integrated supply and trading operation, moved to Dallas.

> "There are certain parts of our business that have to stay operational 24-hours a day, so the magnitude of the storm triggered a move that Thursday before the storm."

"Our Gulf of Mexico remote operations center moved to Dallas with them and was able to share some of the same infrastructure. It's interesting. Because it's a heavily regulated side of the business, we had to move the whole business, human resources and ethics and compliance. Everybody had to go. I think some people took their kids, dogs and everything with them. The move involved over 200 employees.

"We moved into action before the storm made landfall. Our offshore platforms have protocol and stages that are aligned with the rest of industry and government regulations and they went into specified preparatory stages. But since the storm was coming in through Texas, and all our operated platforms are in Louisiana, it was precautionary only.

"We were getting ready, but nobody really knew the magnitude of the storm. I remember Orlando, who's the head of our integrated supply trading group, saying, "It's gonna be a

Category 4', and he was emphatic. And, we were all like, "really?!' But, then, of course it could be true.

"We also have a humanitarian assistance process and a Humanitarian Assistance Team. We had just revised how we would handle helping employees during a crisis. So, we dusted that off and looked at it. It had been rewritten and had gotten kind of transactional. It was about so many dollars per day, call centers, things like that. Mostly of human resources-led type of activities.

"Since my boss, CEO John Mingé, was out of town, I was the acting head of country. So, we looked at all the procedures and policies with human resources and said, 'Well we know where they are, what could trigger what, and decided that we were ready.' But, we didn't quite know ready for what. Like everybody else in south Texas, we watched the storm come in, and weather forecasters were saying this could bring an impressive amount of rain, but I don't think that we ... I didn't internalize that for what it meant."

How could she? Remember Jeff Lindner's account. The weather forecasters were questioning the rainfall output from their own computer models. Who of us could visualize enough rain to fill your backyard with enough water that it reached your neck if you were unfortunate enough to be standing in it. That's the nature of Black Swan events. We'll revisit BP's local response to hurricane Harvey and its aftermath in Chapter 10.

Now, let's look at one individual's unique planning response and the outcome. We've previously met Dr. Cesare Wright in Chapter 6 when we discussed his family's unfortunate rescue experience. Here's the rest of the story.

"We bought our house in Westbury three years ago. It had never flooded, until Tax Day 2016. We got three to five inches of water in the house that day. It took nearly two years to navigate the rebuilding process, dealing with insurance, FEMA, the mortgage company and the contractors. I navigated the process by trial and error. We finished rebuilding from the Tax Day 2016 flood a week before hurricane Harvey arrived. You could see the plastic wrap still on our new stove and refrigerator from literally being installed the day before Harvey arrived.

> "We finished rebuilding from the Tax Day 2016 flood a week before hurricane Harvey arrived. You could see the plastic wrap still on our new stove and refrigerator, from literally being installed the day before Harvey arrived."

"I took hurricane Harvey really seriously. The first time, I was caught unaware because our house had never flooded before. But, when I saw the news and weather reports, it was clear that this storm was going to be epic and a major flood risk. I also knew that the city still hadn't repaired and fully connected the feeder bayous near us to the main bayou.

Water Overflows Three-Foot Dyke

"I had become hypervigilant since the last flood. There were several drainage issues that we'd reported to the city over the past two years. Any time I would notice something that would be a flooding factor, I would report it and ask somebody to fix it. When Harvey arrived, the city still hadn't dealt with those issues.

CHAPTER 8: LEADING FROM THE EYE OF THE STORM

"The week before the flood, I went to Home Depot and bought pallets of gardening soil and compost, about 20,000 pounds, so that I could barricade my house. I anticipated that we would probably get some flooding. Rather than getting sandbags, I opted for the soil because, at the end of the day, what can you do with sand? Make a beach in your backyard?

[Dr. Wright's handiwork appears in the nearby photo. Notice the watermark above the barrier.]

"Potting soil and compost packs down nicely like sand, and later, I could have raised flower beds everywhere. So, if it ended up protecting the house, great. If it doesn't flood, I've just done landscaping. We put three feet of soil bags and plastic around the entire house. That only blocked the initial wave of water. The water rose more than four feet and flooded the house again, despite the barricade.

"That's what I did. I had an obligation to manage my risk of flooding. Doing nothing wasn't an option. Once it flooded, I at least felt comfortable knowing I did everything that I could. I would have felt much worse had I not taken any precautions, had I not tried to do anything and then it flooded."

"We put three feet of soil bags and plastic around the entire house. That only blocked the initial wave of water. The water rose more than four feet and flooded the house again, despite the barricade."

The photo on the next page shows Dr. Wright's dog wearing a life jacket. One of the lessons we can draw from Dr. Wright's experience is that our plans can always be overcome by the unexpected, and especially by the unpredictable. Does that suggest that we shouldn't plan? Is there a difference between planning and pre-

Dog Wearing A LIfejacket

paring? I'll let you consider those questions for a few moments while we examine what Judge Emmett said about planning and learning.

> "We learn from every emergency. You always learn something no matter how well you've got things planned. You're gonna learn something! But in our case, I can't say it often enough. We have a full-time experienced professional staff. We have, probably, the best emergency operation center, both in terms of size and technology, in the country. We have a certain confidence that we're gonna deal with it, whatever it is.
>
> "You know something is always not going to go according to plan. So, you must be able to adjust. The way you do that is to have people who are empowered to make decisions. There can't be a funnel that somebody must go through to make the right decision. And, sometimes those decisions are even outside of Harris County.

"For example, we sent a truck to San Jacinto County to help them set up a shelter. Well, that's not really my responsibility, but it was the right thing to do, and we had somebody on our staff who was able to do that.

We've now read four short stories about planning. Each story featured a different leader, a unique organization, varied planning methods and different results. Yes, Dr. Wright is a leader, and a good one at that. Your first leadership responsibility is leading yourself. But, I digress. What do we learn from these stories?

There are at least three different lessons we can learn or conclusions we can reach. First, plans are almost always overrun by circumstances. Effective plans have built-in mechanisms for coping with this reality. Second, plans are always vulnerable to Black Swan events. Knowing what you don't know is an effective remedy for preventing total failure in Black Swan environments.

Third, plans never survive ineffective leadership. Great plans are never a substitute for poor leadership. On the flipside of that, great leaders can always overcome poor plans because **they believe more in people than plans**. Mayor Turner's leadership approach to overcoming the water and sewer plant crises is a good example.

> ... plans never survive ineffective leadership. Great plans are never a substitute for poor leadership. ... great leaders can always overcome poor plans because **they believe more in people than plans**.

What's the verdict? We've already concluded, contrary to common belief, truth doesn't necessarily have to become a casualty of war. Plans, on the other hand, are always a casualty because none of us can see the future. Effective leadership can always adjust and mitigate planning failures. **Leadership can never survive lies and deceit.**

Fortunately, in the case of hurricane Harvey and its aftermath, we can celebrate victory!

And—The Winners Are...

Us! We the people residing within the area ravaged by hurricane Harvey and its flooding. But, the victory is much larger than that. Our leaders showed the world the results ethically intelligent leadership can produce. By modeling expected behavior, our leaders provided an example for all of us to follow. I can't claim that I know the extent of the effect that example had on the rest of us. But, I agree with Bob Harvey's assessment, the effect was greater than zero. **Leading by example works!** Now we look at sweating underwater.

CHAPTER 9

SWEATING UNDERWATER

Damned if You Do, Damned If You Don't

MEMORIAL AREA COUPLE'S OPEN FLOODGATES STORY

"As the storm was approaching, we weren't terribly alarmed because we've lived in our house 35 years. We've been through hurricanes. We went through a flood in the late 1980s. We had flooded streets, but no water even close to the house. ... We were high and dry. We saw water in the street, but that was it.

"At the start of Harvey's rains, we drove around the neighborhood and looked and saw where the water was, and it was in the expected places. Our house is at the crown of the neighborhood. So, we figured we'd be okay. We were concerned but not worried.

"Mayor Turner was on TV saying, 'If you stay, stay.' So, our attitude was the hurricane's heading to Corpus. We've been through a lot of hurricanes, and we're pretty good at reading flood maps. We knew it was gonna be a water event, and the constant feedback we were getting from public leadership was, 'If you're safe, stay in your home.' So, without fail, everyone stayed in their home. ... Then, ...

"The water suddenly started coming in through the back door. The flow was heavy enough to wrap around my feet. I looked out front. It looked like a fast-flowing river. It was, then, I knew we had to leave the house. We had no warning. No voluntary evacuation. No mandatory evacuation. No notice of any kind. Nothing. It was just—BOOM—the water was gushing in through the backdoor and under the baseboards! Within minutes, we had feet of water in the house!

"Within ten minutes, we had a boat at the front door. We left the neighborhood in the boat carrying a couple of garbage bags of stuff and three cat carriers. We left with one change of clothes and whatever else we could grab in a few minutes. With all the chaos, we couldn't find one cat. So, we left her in the house. Why were we treated this way?"

Fighting The Futility

Carl and Linda were relating their harrowing experience occurring shortly after the Army Corps of Engineers opened the floodgates on the Barker and Addicks reservoir dams. Their story, is one of, at least, 158 stories from their neighborhood. Hurricane Harvey's rains had filled both of those flood-control reservoirs, located on the far west side of Houston, to unprecedented levels, threatening the integrity of both dams.

Meteorologist Jeff Lindner had been on local media talking about the reservoir water levels for a few days before the floodgates were opened. The rapidly rising reservoir water levels shouldn't have been and were not surprising to anyone tuned into local media, including Carl and Linda. Most people downstream of the dams, knew there was a possibility the floodgates might be opened as an emergency measure to prevent failure of the dams.

Instant Flooding in Neighborhood

I thought long and hard about including this matter in this book because it's controversial and the subject of ongoing litigation. Many urged me to leave it out because the book is about Houston's amazing response to hurricane Harvey's flooding and its aftermath, a great positive story. Some consider this event a blemish on that overall story. I agree, it's controversial. I agree it can be construed in a negative way. I agree the incident could be a blemish. Those are compelling points.

But, the forced flooding of those neighborhoods resulting from the dam releases **are part of the story.** Because of the ongoing litigation, the dam releases may be one of the more enduring legacies of the hurricane Harvey Houston story. It must be discussed in this book. There are important lessons available within this controversy. Besides, it provides us with a vehicle for discussing ethical judging.

As we begin this discussion, I want to provide full disclosure.

Carl and Linda are friends and business colleagues of mine. I empathize with what happened to them. But, I can see both sides of this controversy. And, as we say in Texas, I have no dog in this fight. I have no special or "insider" knowledge either.

All the information presented in this chapter, except for my interviews, is publicly available from any number of sources. Finally, it's my fondest hope that the way we look at this dispute, in this chapter, provides a useful framework for future ethical judging opportunities.

Some Background. In 1929 and, again, in 1935, Houston suffered devastating floods from rains falling on the White Oak and Buffalo Bayou watersheds. Out of those catastrophes, arose the Harris County Flood Control District and an Army Corps of Engineers' 1940 plan for addressing the flooding problem. The Barker and Addicks reservoirs represent less than half of that proposed 1940 solution to flooding problem.

Over the passing years, the original flooding problem has grown worse, and its partial solution, the two reservoirs have proven insufficient. The Barker reservoir and dam are a little more than 70 years old. The Addicks reservoir and dam, it's sibling to the north of IH10, is 68 years old. Both dams have been upgraded but are still 70-year-old earthen dams, as depicted in the nearby graphic.

The original 1940 plan had eight elements. All eight elements were needed to handle the **1940s** water runoff, containment and transport problem. These elements were:

1. Barker Reservoir
2. Addicks Reservoir
3. White Oak Reservoir
4. A Containment Levee along Cypress Creek

CHAPTER 9: SWEATING UNDERWATER

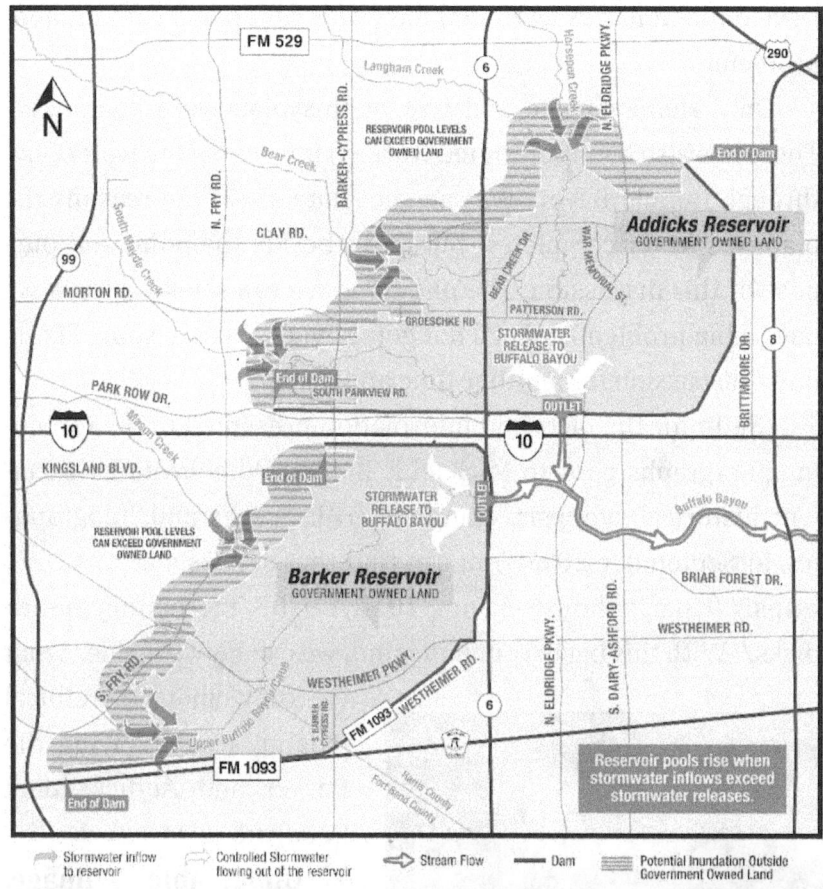

5. Deeping and widening of Buffalo Bayou between what is now Highway 6 and Piney Point
6. A 2-mile-long Brickhouse Gully Bypass Channel
7. A 25-mile-long North channel to the Gulf of Mexico
8. A 35-mile-long South channel to the Gulf of Mexico

The elements of this plan were based on conditions at the time the plan was developed, in the early 1940s. At that time, the entire area was undeveloped prairie, farm and ranch land. Since that time, much of this area has been developed and paved over.

Development has exacerbated the water runoff and containment problem.

Only elements one and two of this plan were completed. There has also been continued work on improving the water flow through Buffalo Bayou. We can speculate about the reasons the plan was never completed, but that's beside the point and purpose of this discussion. The one thing we can say for sure is we have a big problem, and it's not going away anytime soon. Fixing it is a discussion for another time and place.

Credit for the facts and information presented in the foregoing paragraphs goes to Michael F. Bloom. Who wrote an excellent historical synopsis, complete with graphs and infographics, in September 2017. You can find that synopsis at this URL: https://riparianhouston.com/2017/09/03/the-history-of-addicks/. With this background in mind, we can now consider what we know about the ethical judging accompanying the Barker and Addicks dam floodgate releases.

Quickly Flooded Home

Undeniable Damage. The aftermath of those releases is undeniable. More than 4,000 homes and businesses were damaged, some destroyed others damaged less significantly. Families and businesses were and, many still are displaced. Personally, knowing people who were directly impacted by this event gives me a better insight into the human suffering experienced. Even for those whose losses were covered by insurance, the physical and mental toll exacted by the stresses of the event were and continue significant.

CHAPTER 9: SWEATING UNDERWATER

Here is more of Carl and Linda's story.

"Out of one entire week that we went back and forth to our house, we saw one governmental agency. One. It was all volunteers. My son and I went back into our house four times, and finally the last day, caught the last cat and got her out. That was a Saturday. The following Sunday they closed our neighborhood until the water went down, which was the following week.

"By this time, we had two weeks of the house being underwater. Water to your chest. Jumping out of the boat into that muck ... sewage and chemicals, gasoline, oil and gas from the pipelines. The water was gross by then. But, the reason it maintained that 4-foot-plus level was because they kept releasing trillions of gallons from the reservoir into Buffalo Bayou.

"Our house was underwater for a total of three weeks. So, then we had concerns about structural integrity. Could those southeast Texas pine 2x4s support a two-story structure with a tile roof on it? Was it gonna hold? Our front porch cracked from the force of the water.

"The only things we salvaged were upstairs where our kids had lived when they were still at home. Nothing downstairs. All the cars in the neighborhood were left behind because everybody was boated out. Our cars were just left in the garage.

"There was one guy, who was trying to escape from the neighborhood in a small car. It stalled out at the front of the neighborhood and became submerged. Boats kept passing over the top of it. When the water went down, you could see the top of the car where all the boat props had just torn the roof to pieces.

> "We lived in a hotel for a month until we could find an apartment. The first floor of the house is now down to concrete and studs, floor to ceiling. All the plumbing has been removed. It's nothing but the foundation and the 2x4s. I did 90% of that work with a handful of day laborers."

Carl and Linda are independent business owners. They can and do take care of themselves and their family. Having control over their lives instantly snatched from them because of some "bureaucrat" somewhere in the bowels of the government was particularly galling. They continued.

> Relationships are based on truth and trust. We have a relationship with our government. Leadership is all about relationships. Leadership without truth and trust dies.

> "So, what's it been like since? There've been periods of, I think, both of us have gone through melancholy periods. I think we've kind of gotten passed that now. A huge reason for the frustration, disappointment and anger is the way the whole thing was handled. Ultimately, if we were to join a lawsuit, it's because we were so disappointed in the way it was handled.
>
> "If we had had more notice, if they had not turned off our power, we would have known something from the TV. If we had known more, if we had known what we know today we would have done things completely differently than we did. I feel like they just pulled the plug. It was so poorly handled to dump that kind of water on anybody."

As you might glean from Jason and Tammy's story, it's one thing to suffer from an unavoidable natural calamity such as hurricane

Harvey. That's bad enough, but over time we pick ourselves up and get over it. It's something entirely different when we believe much of our suffering and stress could have been avoided had we been privy to all the available information.

This lack of transparency tested our trust in government leaders, at all levels, because, as Judge Eckels observed, we tend to merge all levels of government into a single entity called "government." Relationships are based on truth and trust. We have a relationship with our government. Leadership is all about relationships. Leadership without truth and trust dies. Let's examine what we know, or think we know about the truth of this situation.

Testing Our Trust

During the past seven months, as I've researched and written this book, I've talked to multiple dozens of people both public officials and others. When the issue of opening the Barker and Addicks floodgates arises, I've gotten widely varying stories about who made the final decision, when it was made and why there was no prior communication to the public about the imminent flooding.

Invariably, the question arises as to when our local public officials knew about the decision to open the floodgates, depicted in the nearby picture. Again, there are differences of opinion as to whether our local public officials knew in advance of the decision to open the floodgates and whether those same officials knew anything about the timing.

The answer is binary. It should be simply—yes or no. If yes, when was the information made available to our public officials? I received a direct answer to this question from Mayor Turner. When we talked, it was at a large conference table, and the conversation included several members of the Mayor's team. All of them agreed with the Mayor's account.

Here's part of my conversation with the mayor.

> **John:** "What was your darkest moment during the emergency?"
>
> **Mayor Turner:** "When the Corps [US Army Corp of Engineers] released the water without providing us notice and, then, people's homes started flooding. We had a situation where a lot of people in the west Houston area were refusing to leave their homes. Even when a voluntary request was made, they didn't want to leave their homes.
>
> "At the same time, we had firefighters and other first responders attending to the people's needs out in that flood water. My leadership team came to me on Friday morning and said they were out there responding to calls for help, but the power was still on. The houses were flooded, and the first responders could feel the tingling [from the live electrical wires] in their boots.
>
> What they said to me was, 'Mayor, this is a dangerous situation. Not only for the people who are choosing to stay in their homes, but for those of us first responders who are trying to meet their needs.'"
>
> **John:** "So, the Corps didn't give anybody notice they were going to start flooding houses?"
>
> **Mayor Turner:** "The Corps said they were going to release about 4,000 cubic feet per second from Addicks and about the same from Barker. It was going to be a gradual release to get

up to about 8,000 cubic feet per second. They didn't indicate to what degree that level of release would cause people's homes to flood, but they said they were doing a gradual release.

"Later on, in the wee hours of the morning, they made a decision to go beyond that level. Instead of it being 8,000, they made the decision to go up to 14,000. That decision was made in the wee hours of the morning. In a news release the next day, the Corps announced they had unexpectedly released large volumes. Well, thanks for letting us know!

"So, the point is, we didn't know about it, and there was no magnitude to determine to what degree people's home were going to flood. Once those homes started flooding that created a whole set of issues."

John: So, people blaming you because you asked people not to evacuate is totally bogus. I've talked to a lot of those people in west Houston, and they're blaming you because, 'The mayor told us to stay in our house.'

Mayor Turner: "Not only me but the County Judge [Judge Ed Emmett] as well."

John: "I am glad to find this out."

Mayor Turner: "The people's homes in west Houston didn't flood because of the rain that fell from the sky. Thousands of homes flooded because of the flood gate release."

John: "I've been told that the decision was made in Washington. Do you have that same impression?"

Mayor Turner: "When I talked to the Corps on the phone, they said they had their own set of protocols. They said, 'Mayor, we follow our protocols.' When I asked them, 'Well, why don't you gradually reduce what you are doing such that the flood waters can recede and people can get out of the areas? Then, once the people are out, you can increase again.'

> "The Corps made it very clear to me that they had their own set of protocols. They followed their protocols. And, the city of Houston would have no impact, no decision-making authority with them. So, if people want to blame the City or blame me, they need to look someplace else."

Hold your thoughts on this conversation. We'll return to the mayor's story in just a moment. I want to add some additional context to this story. I've heard many comments about the electricity being shut off just prior to the water release from the dams. Some have cited this "fact" as a way of proving "everyone" knew what was coming. Here's what Executive Assistant Fire Chief Mann had to say.

> "Our rescue teams were out in the areas flooded by the dam releases. We needed to verify that we had all the people out. We were going door-to-door in the water. Some places with water over your head. Some, water to the roofline. So, we were making a house-by-house search.
>
> "We were using poles to tap on windows. Just making sure that if there was anybody there, we were getting them out. Obviously, this was mainly on that west side evacuation area. Our teams were reporting back that they were feeling electrical tingles because the water was being electrified and they could feel...especially the USAR teams had dry suits on, they could still feel the electrical charge in the water.
>
> "We worked with CenterPoint trying to isolate the source. Our teams were reporting that the street lights were still on.

The porch lights were still on and the water's up over the window sill. and their porch light is on. So, we came back and we took that information and evaluated the extreme risks that out teams were taking to accomplish the mission that we had given them, which was to verify that search and rescue of that area was complete."

What does this additional context add to our understanding of the situation? The power wasn't simply turned off for the impacted areas before the water release began. Chief Mann said it was a surprise to him and his team that the electrical current was still flowing when he dispatched his search and rescue teams. Incidentally, they had to check on 125,000 houses! Now back to the mayor.

Was the Mayor Turner telling the truth? I think he was and still is. I could be wrong. I've been wrong before. But, I've been around the block a few times. I started out my professional career as an auditor. I've heard more than a few tall tales over the years. It's not easy to pull the wool over my eyes. But, there's another more important consideration factoring into my conclusion.

> Logically, Mayor Turner had everything to lose and little to gain by allowing all those homes to flood with no notice to the people living in them.

Logically, Mayor Turner had everything to lose and little to gain by allowing all those homes to flood with no notice to the people living in them. Creating the anger, frustration and litigation we now see doesn't resound to any public official's benefit. The community anger and frustration levels could have been much less under a mandatory evacuation order. Despite that logical case, however; we see widespread mistrust.

You might ask the question, "So what!" This is nothing new. Our Founding Fathers warned us about political parties and lying politicians. I agree. This is nothing new. But, is it a good situation? Why does it matter, anyway?

It matters because, like it or not, we all have a relationship with our public officials. What they do and how they do it impacts our lives. Remember, leadership fails when there is no truth and trust in the leadership relationship. We should care about this problem. But, we should care as much or more about how these ethical judgments are made. The strategies used in these cases is critical. So, let's examine ethical judging strategies, generally, and those used in this case.

Sweating the Strategy

Ethical judging strategies have been in a downward spiral toward insanity for millennia. Where once we holistically assessed ethical dilemmas, considering the people involved and the specific situations and contexts, we now open a rulebook, thumb to the rule that most closely fits the dilemma, and then, blindly pronounce an ethical judgment based on whatever the rule says.

When questioned about some of the outrageous outcomes produced by this strategy, we innocently throw our hands up in the air and say, "I had no choice. That's what the rule says." Or, we say, "We have our protocols." Let's consider an all-too-familiar story.

Our Rules-Based Zero-Tolerance Society. Tim was sitting in a Monday afternoon staff meeting watching a PowerPoint presentation, given by a Compliance Department lawyer, concerning the company's zero-tolerance policy on sexual harassment. As a senior manager, Tim was required to take this course every quarter as one of his KPIs. The first slide of the presentation was about #MeToo.

The company policy was well documented, had been around for several years and required a series of 18 action steps *any* time an **allegation** of sexual harassment arose in his department. The policy didn't allow any contexts or circumstances consideration. The only requirement for activating the entire policy segment and investigation was an **allegation**, serious or otherwise.

As a senior manager, Tim had discretion in all other areas of his responsibilities, including hiring and firing, promotions, performance, multi-million budgets and P&L. In this one area, he had no discretion. All it took, for the entire cascade of unpleasant events waterfall to occur, was an allegation of inappropriate behavior.

> The only requirement for activating the entire policy segment and investigation was an **allegation**, serious or otherwise.

In the past two years, there had been three instances of innocent misunderstandings that could have been handled with a frank discussion and some adult behavior. He couldn't ever have that discussion. The policy was the policy.

As a result, he, and most of his peers, hated to hear anyone mention anything about sexual harassment as it meant a long intrusive investigation, which 99 times out of 100 resulted in nothing but department discord, disruption and dissent. As the lawyer droned on, Tim noticed a text appear on his phone. It was from his wife Jan.

The text read, "Call me! We have a problem!" Tim quietly excused himself from the meeting, slipped out and called his wife. Jan immediately answered the phone and was angry and upset. She said, "Lacey has been expelled from school. That toy squirt gun we bought her at the waterpark on Sunday was still in her backpack and fell out in class.

"Her teacher immediately took her to the principal's office. The principal called me to come pick her up from school. The principal explained to me the school had a zero-tolerance policy for guns on campus and expulsion was mandatory. Kasey has been expelled for a week for bringing a gun to school.

"When I tried to explain that it was simply a toy water gun, the principal told me to 'be careful' because he could call the police, which, in most cases, was required under the policy. He told me to be grateful Kacey was being allowed to come back to school."

Tim's initial reaction was to go to school and unload on the principle for being a jackass—what is a zero-tolerance policy that allows for no exceptions, that allows for no common sense? His thought process was interrupted by the zero-tolerance sexual harassment meeting breaking up!

Mindless Strategies. Before we start this discussion, let me say I regard both issues as intrinsically serious. Sexual harassment of any kind and in any setting should never be tolerated. Likewise, students bringing weapons to school is a serious matter and shouldn't be allowed. I use both issues as examples because everybody reading this book is familiar with both. My problem is the ethical judging strategies our society now imposes trivializes whatever issue to which the strategy is applied. Let me explain how we got here.

As we get started, I want to establish a distinction in terms. If you are unfamiliar with my work in this area, you may be wondering why I'm using the term judging instead of decision-making. The reason is simple. I make a distinction between people and things. In my worldview, people are more important than things.

We make decisions about where to eat lunch, what car to buy and where to live. These decisions all involve things. There is a reason we have judges in our legal system and not decision-makers. When you're assessing an ethical dilemma, your judging outcomes are going to affect people. So, the distinction is easy. Judging affects people. Decision-making affects things.

Ethical judging is at the core of our ethical intelligence. Ethical judging is one of the most important things we do because our ethical judgments directly affect people's lives. Whenever we're assessing an ethical dilemma we're evaluating the outcomes of our potential choices. Those outcomes often change someone's life either for the better or for the worse. The strategy, or the process, we use is critical. How did we get here?

The Death of Reason. Francis Bacon gave us the Scientific Method, a different way of objectively evaluating and understanding reality. René Descartes gave us the dual nature of humanity and an ethical calculus. Immanuel Kant completed Descartes's calculus with his categorical imperative. These artifacts of the Enlightenment signaled the death knell for holistic ethical judging, the prevailing ethical judging process for almost four millennia.

Since the Enlightenment, Western society has embraced science and technology. We've tried, and in many cases, succeeded in reducing life and important human judgments to algorithms run on a computer. We've almost reached the point, where we humans don't trust ourselves anymore. We put more faith in what an ostensibly "objective" computer program tells us than our own human judgment.

This has become especially true in large organizations. Leadership of those organizations would rather trust ethical judging to policies, processes, procedures and rulebooks. Instead of creating and fostering ethically intelligent cultures where organizational members are encouraged to make ethical judgments, often called doing the right thing, because the culture dictates it, these leaders resort to these zero-tolerance formulas.

This is how we get second graders expelled from school for accidentally bringing a harmless water pistol in her backpack. This is how we get innocent students expelled from college because of formulaic Title IX proceedings. And, **this is also how we get floodgates on dams opened in the middle of the night without warning.**

I am sure the "bureaucrat" who made the decision to open the dams without notice was just following policies, procedures and rules, the "protocol." We shouldn't blame him or her. We should look into the mirror to fix the blame. We elect people. And, then, we allow them to make life or death judgments in dark rooms with little or no oversight.

> We've almost reached the point, where we humans don't trust ourselves anymore. We put more faith in what an ostensibly "objective" computer program tells us than our own human judgment.

Ethical judging must be done holistically by a responsible human who is, then, held accountable for that judgment's aftermath.

Now, let's return to the celebrating!

CHAPTER 10

CELEBRATING GOODNESS

Opening Night for La Traviata in the Resilience Theater

La Traviata, is an opera by Giuseppe Verdi that was first performed in 1853 and is set in 18th century Paris. La Traviata was the first opera performed by the Houston Grand Opera from the Resilience Theater, also known as Salon A3 of the George R. Brown Convention Center, located in downtown Houston. Here are a few lyrics from early in the first act.

> **ALFREDO**
> *Drink from the joyful glass,*
> *resplendent with beauty,*
> *drink to the spirit of pleasure*

which enchants the fleeting moment.
Drink to the thrilling sweetness
brought to us by love,
for these fair eyes, irresistibly,
pierce us to the heart.
Drink - for wine
will warm the kisses of love.

ALL

Drink - for wine
will warm the kisses of love.

VIOLETTA

I shall divide my gaiety
among you all;
Everything in life is folly,
except for pleasure.
Let us be joyful, for love
is a fleeting and short-lived joy.
A flower which blossoms and fades,
whose beauty is soon lost forever.
Be joyful - a caressing voice
invites us warmly to joy.

Lyrics available at: http://www.murashev.com/opera/La_traviata_libretto_English_Italian

These lyrics speak of love, joy and the evanescence of life's moments. During hurricane Harvey many of us recalled some of our most joyous life events, a recall sparked by seeing Harvey's flood waters consume artifacts of those memories. Memories are not just one-dimensional pictures. Memories are stored and

CHAPTER 10: CELEBRATING GOODNESS

recalled as packages of sights, sounds, smells and emotions.

Having our emotions aroused heightened our awareness of the primacy of people over things. We called, texted or posted, reaching out to the important people in our lives. When our house was surrounded by multiple feet of water, our daughter was insistent on coming to rescue us. It was only after my wife texted pictures of boats and helicopters rescuing neighbors was our daughter's rescue ardor cooled.

These events rekindled our love for one another as we empathized with one another. We saw in the images of suffering strangers our fathers, mothers, brothers, sisters, sons, daughters and other family members. We felt their pain and sorrow as never before. We volunteered in record numbers. We prayed. We commiserated. We tried to help in any way we could.

> We felt their pain and sorrow as never before. We volunteered in record numbers. We prayed. We commiserated. We tried to help in any way we could.

I decided to write this book so that we would have a record of this life-changing experience. My research brought many people across my path who had suffered great loss. Their tears became my tears, their pain my pain. My sorrow became so deep, I had to block it from dissolving my joy. There was sorrow enough to go around. Joy needed amplification.

> Their tears became my tears, their pain my pain. My sorrow became so deep, I had to block it from dissolving my joy. There was sorrow enough to go around. Joy needed amplification.

For most of us, the arts is an amplifier of joy. Who can forget *Ode to Joy*? I've downloaded 12 different renditions! Whether it's music, opera, ballet, cinema, country western dancing or wrestling (rasslin' in some parts), the aesthetic part of our humanity helps us bring or restore our joy. Yes, I think country western dancing and wrestling are art forms! Have you ever tried doing either? I didn't think so. But, I digress.

During the weeks after the water receded and house mucking in sweltering homes without air conditioning was the activity du jour, I happened to see a news report about the Houston Grand Opera and the devastating flood damage to its venue, the Wortham Theater. I also noted that its director announced they were looking for an alternate venue so that the 2017-18 season could go on uninterrupted. I thought, *what a crazy but wonderful idea!*

As I let that crazy idea—rebuilding an opera company weeks before opening night—sink into my mind, I had an epiphany! Our opera company was embodying the community spirit I was seeing, a spirit that says, "We've got this! We're going to pick ourselves up out of this mud and muck and get on with it! What we do is important in this community! We've got to help our community get its joy back!" At that moment, I knew I had to talk to the person behind this crazy plan!

Seeing the Spirit

A few days before Christmas 2017, I went to visit with Houston Grand Opera (HGO) Managing Director, Perryn Leech in HGO's temporary offices, which were nicely appointed and located in a borrowed space in downtown Houston. We've previously met Director Leech back in Chapter 5 when we discussed living a life driven by purpose.

I opened our conversation with my observation about how he, HGO and his plan for rebuilding the opera company so exemplified the spirit of the people who live in this metropolitan area specifically and in Texas, generally. I also asked him to reflect on his darkest moment and his reasoning behind pushing so hard for completing the 2017-18 season in a single venue.

> "I'm just massively proud of this city and this opera company. Particularly, the way this city hasn't let the tragedy ... I saw [hurricane] Katrina being reported from UK, and the reporting very much was about victims and how the city [New Orleans] was broken ... The reporting here was never about how the city [Houston] was broken. It was about the strength of the city, and the willingness of its people to work together.
>
> "For example, there was a guy with a flat bottom boat who was out there saving people. He delivered a pregnant lady to the medical district because there was enough water on Holcombe for him to take her down to the hospital, and she had her baby there.
>
> "That's why I like Houston, and that's why we came to Houston. The spirit and the can-do attitude of the people here. To see that spirit and also see the immediate way our board responded just hugely magnified everyone's resolve. ...
>
> "We said we're going to have a Harvey relief fund for staff who had been badly affected and got to nearly $90,000 in that fund in very short order because people were like... 'This is our company, and we're going to help support people getting back on their feet. It's been an amazing four months. All the good qualities of Houston have shone through like no other time.
>
> "That's why I love being in the city and that's why I'm proud to be a member of the community here and bring what I think is a really great arts company. It's worth fighting for and worth saying, 'We got kicked. We're up. We're going to keep walking forward because we have no choice.'"

Although I've lived in Houston much longer than Director Leech, we're both transplants, me from Michigan and Director Leech from the United Kingdom. Despite our different backgrounds, we've both become Texans and Houstonians. That designation includes a set of personal attributes, not the least of which is a "can do, up-from-the-boot-straps attitude."

You can knock us down. We'll get right back up. Shake ourselves off. Perhaps, say a few choice words, not fit to print here. Then, get "back into the saddle," and try again. We don't let yesterday steal today. We don't dwell on the setback. We learn and move on. That attitude is reflected in Director Leech's response to a question about dark moments.

> "We're fighting every single day to keep the people coming to the opera, which segues nicely into the last four months. I've no knowledge of an opera company that's ever taken a season off and come back and been successful."

> "My darkest moment? I'm not someone who dwells for long on dark moments. I have a one foot in front of the other psychology that doesn't allow me to dwell on mistakes and on things that are beyond my control. Certainly, walking into the Wortham for the first time and realizing ... I'd sort of been cushioned slightly because I'd been to the Alley Theater beforehand and then went to the Wortham. Having seen the Alley, I kind of knew what I was going to be walking into. ...

> "We're fighting every single day to keep the people coming to the opera, which segues nicely into the last four months. I've no knowledge of an opera company that's ever taken a season off and come back and been successful. It just doesn't happen. There are multiple examples, the New York City opera being a very good one.

"When the Koch Theater closed for refurbishment, it was the New York City opera's death knell. They tried to go around New York City and find different venues for productions. People will never buy subscriptions for that for sure. And, ours is still a relatively heavy subscription model. People don't like to be messed around like that.

"In a recent media interview, I said the worst thing that could happen is ten years from now we could be asking, 'Do you remember the great arts companies we used to have before Harvey?' Because we are certainly in a position for that to happen.

"The losses for the whole Theatre District are around $60 million and that's before we can get into repairing the Wortham Theater and Jones Hall. Ours is between $12 and $15 million. The Alley is around $20 million, and then there are the others who also have significant losses.

"Those are very significant losses. [Wortham Theatre damage in nearby photo] But, none of us [in the Arts community] are going to say, 'Well that's what it is. Let's just downscale.' That's not what this city is about. That's not what we do! It's worth fighting for!"

My response to that is—BRAVO! Here, we see in this one man and this one organization a shining example of the undying spirit of the community that is the Houston metropolitan area. We never give in. We never give up. We don't allow our circumstances to dictate our destiny. That's how we not only survive but thrive in the third largest city in the country, which is built in a place that all logic says NO WAY! But, the Allen brothers said, "YES WAY!" They built and we continue building because we never see ourselves as victims, even with the flooded kitchen in the nearby photo.

Victors Not Victims

A Texas Renaissance Man Speaks.

"I grew up in place called Cut and Shoot, Texas. We lived in a trailer with a few broken windows. I learned how to live simply. I learned how to hunt and fish and could live off the land if I had to. You could take away my cell phone, laptop and all the other gadgets I use in my work, and I'd be okay. Give me a one room cabin with a roof over my head, and I could easily live off the land. You could take all of these modern things away from me, including even electricity, and I would be fine."

I was talking to a man whose home was ravaged by hurricane Harvey's floodwaters. He had just finished rebuilding his home from the floodwaters of the "Tax Day" flood of 2016. In fact, he told me he still had the boxes his new appliances had come in still in his garage. In the nearby photo you can see the packing material still attached to a new stove. The short story I related was taken from a conversation he had with opposing legal counsel in a lawsuit some years ago.

To get him to drop his lawsuit, the opposing counsel threatened to take everything he owned and destroy his life if he didn't drop the lawsuit. His remarks to the opposing counsel are symbolic of a fierce spirit of independence we Texans possess, including native-born and those who got here as fast as we could.

Before you jump to conclusions and assume those remarks came from an individual who had "not much to lose," let me disabuse you of that thought. This is a man who was educated at some of the finest institutions our country has to offer, had traveled the world and built a successful career. No, he had a lot to lose when he made those remarks to the opposing legal counsel. It was his Texan "badassness" coming out.

In her book, *Cut'n Shoot, Texas: The Roy Harris Story*, Robin Montgomery said, "Cut'n Shoot ... is more than just a town of world renown. It is a state of mind reflective of a readiness to fight for one's beliefs while respecting a reasonable compromise."

> "I was impressed by how Houstonians were not victims. You see disasters around the world, and people are waiting for the government to come save them. Not here!"

Our state of mind and heart is the key to our current and future behavior. Proverbs 23:7 says, "For as he thinks in his heart, so is he." A common theme running through all the conversations I've had with people while researching this book can be summarized as, "We/I don't think that way!" Here's a good example from Scott Crowder, KTRH NewsRadio Anchor and Reporter.

"I was impressed by how Houstonians were not victims. You see disasters around the world, and people are waiting for the government to come save them. Not here! People were out in boats and donating all kinds of money and bringing food. We got so much food brought to the radio station, it was like almost everyday restaurants were falling all over themselves to serve us food. And I know they were doing that with all the first responders too."

Your Thinking determines your destiny because it governs your attitude. Attitude is a success or failure driver. Granted, there are many other factors that determine success or failure. These include talent, education, personality, connections and others. In my experience, attitude tops all of these. When I'm hiring a new team member, give me someone with a positive can-do attitude and, even if there is a deficit in other factors, I'll choose attitude every time over talent, education and, even, connections.

> Bad attitudes are worse than a bad cold. Attitude is infectious. … One person with a negative attitude can poison an entire group of people. … In these parts, we have a victorious attitude because we are victors and never victims.

When I'm coaching and mentoring, I teach that victory begins in the mind. A victorious attitude is prerequisite to winning. Students will walk into one of my accounting, finance or statistics courses and say something like, "I'm terrible with numbers. I'm really going to struggle in this course." My immediate response to them is, "I agree, you're doomed!"

They'll look at me with this incredulous look on their face and ask me, "How can you say such a thing!" That exchange gives me the opportunity to talk about how victory begins in the mind and

CHAPTER 10: CELEBRATING GOODNESS

attitude determines your success. My approach to this subject often surprises my business clients, especially those who've had setbacks. Bad attitudes are worse than a bad cold.

Attitude is infectious. You might recall we talked about the idea of "limbic lock" a few chapters back. One person with a negative attitude can poison an entire group of people. On the other hand, one person with a positive, uplifting and hopeful attitude can transform an entire department. In these parts, we have a victorious attitude because we are victors and never victims.

Bob Harvey, President & CEO of the Greater Houston Partnership, was comparing the aftermath of hurricane Harvey in Houston and the aftereffects of hurricane Katrina's refugee influx into Houston in 2005. During that emergency, more than a quarter of a million people from New Orleans came to Houston within just a few days. He had these comments.

> "After the fact when people talk about their personal experience of being that person rescued, it's again...contrasting it with New Orleans where from the very beginning people were acting like the government had to come in and somehow solve the problems. And there seemed to be no default to individual initiative, individual responsibility, what can we do to help ourselves and others. And, I admit, we're a more asset-rich community than New Orleans. So, things that we can do would be hard for New Orleans. But still, attitudinally, what a difference!"
>
> "It serves as a good reminder that a single individual initiative multiplied by 100,000 times ends up producing incredible results. Something that could not really have been done any other way. There's no way we had the official resources— the sheriff's department and the fire department or the na-

tional guard. There was simply no way they were going to get in there and rescue those people."

There's another thinking distinction I also want to make. Your thinking is a significant factor in awakening, nurturing and maturing your ethical intelligence. But I'm not talking about thinking in general. I'm talking about the *type of thinking* that occupies your mind. Please don't be offended, but most people are small thinkers. Their thoughts are focused on the minutia. Their mind is overrun with details.

Small thinkers make their way through this minutia much like someone who is hiking through a forest walks through and among the trees. All they see are the individual trees and the surrounding details. Don't get me wrong, there is nothing wrong with this kind of thinking, but it's *not* the kind of thinking that leads to an ethically intelligent life.

In addition to the ability to engage in small thinking, ethically intelligent people are big thinkers. Big thinkers are strategic thinkers. They disengage from the details and look at the big picture. It's the classical 30,000-foot metaphor we use when we describe CEO thinking.

Big thinkers can construct the context and connect the dots. They see the gems in the coal dust. Big thinkers can see the miracle in the mess. Big thinkers are what we call general systems thinkers or, using the more modern terminology, holistic thinkers. We used to believe this was left-versus right-brain thinking.

I'm not so sure of that simple answer anymore. I prefer to call it whole brain thinking. Why is this important?

It's important because ethical dilemmas occur within relationships—often a mosaic of relationships. In many cases, those relationships overlap and create subsets of equitable claims. The ethically intelligent person must be able to grasp the entirety of the situation and be able to connect dots of information that, on the surface, seem unrelated. That kind of superficial analysis is insufficient for rendering equitable ethical judgments.

Harris County Sheriff Ed Gonzalez addressed this idea when we discussed his department's storm response preparations. Here's what he had to say.

> *"We prepare for the worst, but we hope for the best. While nothing prepares you for a storm like Harvey, I think that my collective experience was useful. I had served as mayor pro tem for the city of Houston as well as being through weather events and thinking in a global perspective.*
>
> *"To me, leadership a lot of times, it's not always you doing everything, but just having a good understanding of where resources are and how to deploy them, which means connecting the right people and connecting the dots that connect the dots. It's having that 30,000-foot view saying let's think of as many contingency plans as we can.*
>
> *"We have to be nimble because we can't be married to one particular strategy or deployment model. We have to be open to everything. It's a matter of communicating, not insulating myself and getting people involved and being inclusive so everybody is at the table and can add their expertise. Then, delegate to them.*
>
> *"This is what we want and expect. The flow of communi-*

cations is going to be important. All these factors have helped me get prepared for this. And again, at the end of the day it just speaks to the resilient nature of our region and public safety in general. Our professionals. This is what they signed up for—helping people."

And, help we did! We're going to close this chapter and book with more stories of uplifting the good.

Lifting the Good

The original title of this book was Breathing Goodness, a title I chose even while we were still coping with the aftermath of the storm. My selection was based on what I was seeing—an incredible display of human goodness. We subsequently changed the title for descriptive purposes, but the original observation still stands. We're going to lift additional stories of goodness, beginning with one of Houston's corporate citizens. We pick up our conversation with Cindy Yeilding, Senior Vice President BP America.

> "We live on Buffalo Bayou. Our neighbor called us at about 3:00 AM Sunday and said, 'According to the USGS flood gauges and the predictions they're making, there's a good chance that all of our houses are going to flood.'
>
> "So, we got up and started moving the furniture. About 8:00 AM, I got on the phone with our Houston HR Vice President, Helena Fyda—who was just fantastic. I just can't celebrate her enough. I was talking with Helena, she was in the Heights. So, she was experiencing a little bit of rain, but staying literally high and dry. I'm like, it's getting a little crazy here on Buffalo Bayou. The water is rising and rising.

Flooding Outside a BP America Houston Office

"We started watching the weather reports. By Sunday afternoon we had water in places we've never seen water. By late Sunday we had over six feet of water in our street. We didn't even know there was topography on our street! Water coming in under the house and still rising. Helena and I were talking at about 4:00 in the afternoon. I could picture her wadding up our response plan and saying, "We gotta start over!' The nearby photo shows water outside one of BP's Houston offices.

"That Sunday we decided to trigger our humanitarian assistance process. We, then realized, that if the flooding were to continue at the rate we were seeing, we were poorly positioned to respond to it based in Houston. Fortunately, we have a crisis center in Naperville, Illinois near the south side of Chicago. We made the call. It was a easy one to make—to stand up our humanitarian assistance team in Chicago.

"We put the authority and the leadership of that team in Chicago. So, it was super-clear that we had someone dedicat-

BP America Houston Office Complex

ed to our response. That involved setting up a call center and staffing it with people who could advise on available employee resources. We gave the call center the list of resources available for BP employees who were impacted in any way by the storm. That included some per diems, resources for car rentals, help with different things.

"So, we started brainstorming. Suppose someone's house floods. What's the most important thing to do? It's to start the mucking out process and the remediation. The initial response is critical to be able to recover your house. if we really want to help people through this and help get them back to work, would that service be of help? HR in Chicago began investigating what that sort of support might look like. The nearby photo shows water outside one of BP's Houston offices.

"In the meantime, our employees all started helping one other. And this was...I'm sure that you've heard these stories repeatedly, but people start to use BP social media trying to find who needed help. People were getting together. All over

CHAPTER 10: CELEBRATING GOODNESS

Flooded BP America Houston Facility

Houston we were starting to put volunteers with the people who needed them.

"People started opening up their homes. I think a lot of people just had people rotating through. Just like all of Houston. That was neat. By Monday, several people's homes had flooded and we realized this was unprecedented and getting overwhelming. Then I guess it was Monday afternoon or Tuesday that it sort of hit us ... this is bad.

We triggered money on Monday. I've never seen us move $750,000 so fast. But I said, 'We need to give money. And said, here, here, here, give it.' And we did. I was shocked. I have never seen us send money out to the United Way, the Mayor's fund, and Red Cross that fast!"

Even though BP America is part of a huge multinational organization, Cindy and her team quickly mobilized a comprehensive Houston response, administered from Chicago. That response ultimately helped at least 950 out of 4,500 local BP America employees. BP bore the entire expense of hiring Serve-Pro, a nationwide remediation firm, to restore these employee's homes.

At the time of our interview in January 2018, hundreds of employees were still off work and receiving full salaries. All during Cindy's work helping others, her own home was in a badly flooded area. She remarked that her front yard was on national news on several occasions. In the meanwhile, BP America's Houston facilities suffered severe damage. When I visited in January 2018, staff was still operating in temporary facilities. Cindy and her team at BP America stepped up and did what was right when it was most needed.

Often, tragic events like hurricane Harvey, lead us to reflect on some of our own beliefs about the world. Bob Harvey, President & CEO of the Greater Houston Partnership made this insightful observation. The nearby photo shows water outside one of BP's Houston offices.

> "So, I feel like I've learned some personal lessons from watching this happen—I've got to be more respectful of the non-institutional aspect of community engagement. The culture matters. It matters even at the community level. We saw it during the Super Bowl, the outpouring of Houstonians supporting the Super Bowl in February 2017, as volunteers, playing various roles on the street, representing the community.
>
> "We stopped accepting volunteers at 10,000. We could only handle 10,000, but there were so many more. There is something about this community and our people's willingness and desire to support and be proud of our community. Then, we saw it again eight months later in a totally different way. But it was a similar manifestation of civic pride, civic engagement just plain goodness. Our people asked the question,

'How can I be helpful even if I'm just one person?' Being just one is okay.

"There is something remarkable in what people around the country are saying. They're saying what we have here is unique. They're either saying, 'My community would not have responded that way.' Or, they're asking themselves, 'I wonder if my community would have responded that way.' It's good that they're at least asking the question. That's a good way to start."

Never Sell Yourself Short. We should never underestimate the power of **US**! No, that isn't an acronym for our country, although it could be. No, us means you and me and everyone else who lives in this community, state and country. We demonstrated the power of us when we decided to act right and help one another during hurricane Harvey, irrespective of our "tribe." Here's another example of what one person's initiative and heroic actions can accomplish.

Willie Rios is Mayor *pro tem*, of the City of South Houston. His mayoral duties are only part time. When he's not acting as a public servant, Willie is owner/operator of his own construction and service company.

"The storm hit us hard that night [Saturday, the 26th] about 11:00 pm. We got about 30 inches of water in an hour and a half. Our city took in the most water its ever taken in. We were watching the Mayweather fight. I went outside because the cable kept on going off. When I got outside, we already had six or eight inches of standing water. So, I moved my cars to higher ground, and I told my wife I'm gonna go and check on my dad.

"There was no way to get to him using a car. The water was rising fast. I went on my tractor. On my way to my dad's,

which was six blocks away, people stopped me at the community center. Within 30 minutes we had 14 inches of water. Within another 15 minutes, water rose to where the whole city was flooded. We declared a state of emergency. I think we were one of the first cities that actually declared...the storm just hovered over us for the right amount of time."

You might recall, in Chapter 8, I mentioned the collective epiphany that occurred in this metropolitan area regarding the storm. Willie was part of that epiphany. He realized that he and his brother-in-law were it. There was no other help coming. He continued.

"Once I realized how bad it was, I started rescuing people. Not that I wanted to do it or that I wouldn't do it, but I had to do it because our police cars couldn't get out there. Some of them flooded right away. And, the ones that weren't flooded couldn't make it outside the police station. By that time, we had a foot and a half to two feet of water. The fire trucks were lost right away. They flooded out around midnight.

"The only source of rescue was me and my brother-in-law who was helping. People were calling the [Harris County] Sheriff for help in South Houston. He and I are good friends. So, he called me. By 1:00 AM, I was going to people and picking them up because, in some places there was three to four feet of water, especially in the low spots of the city. My tractor was the only vehicle that could make it through the water.

"When it started, I thought it would be one or two phone calls. But, the calls never stopped. All night I kept getting phone calls from people because I know so many people in town. I was born and raised in the city of South Houston so I know every single street. I either fell down, or rode a bike *down, or learned how to drive on these streets. So, I know the city really well. ...*

"We had a lot of people that needed help. But, the tractor has limited room. When we got to a house we would park it to go into the house and find the people. I would put the bucket down so all the water wouldn't hit the battery or the engine. I would leave the engine running fast. The water was up to my chest on some houses. You know, four and five feet of water in some houses. They were real low. Close to the bayou. And, you couldn't see the roads. Man, on some of them you could barely see the mailbox!"

These conditions were extremely dangerous. Driving a tractor in darkness surrounded by water that is four-foot-deep would seem like driving across a lake using a tractor. Willie was fully aware of the risks. Yet, he kept going. He picks up the story, again.

"But, like I said, I grew up in the city so I know every single inch. It was scary. We went through a mini-tornado while we were rescuing people. We had God on our side. The tornado started funneling the water and the trash right in front of us. We hunkered down next to a gas station. That's when I had the most people on the tractor.

"I had 14 people, including myself on the tractor as we waited next to that gas station for the tornado to pass by. That was one of the most life-threatening experiences I've ever had. I was scared parked next to that gas

> "I had 14 people, including myself on the tractor as we waited next to that gas station for the tornado to pass by. That was one of the most life-threatening experiences I've ever had. I was scared parked next to that gas station."

station. It was all real, but I began thinking...you know you are trying to help people. But if all these people die, you lose. Then, your purpose is really defeated."

I hope you're enjoying and appreciating reading about this man's heroism as much as I had researching and writing about it. I want to briefly interrupt Willie's compelling story to add a bit of context. Hurricane Harvey made landfall at Rockport, Texas on Friday the 25th. It was moving slowly northeast, and the tropical force winds, by that Saturday night, had reached the city of South Houston. So, while you're reading this his narrative, keep in mind that tropical force winds were blowing the rain sideways as they're watching the tornado pass by them. Now, we continue.

"I was thinking, You shouldn't be doing it. You're putting more in harm's way than it's helping them.... But people kept calling me. A family called. They were located off Peacock, a street, that was under four or five feet of water. We went in there. We rescued two new-borns, one seven-year-old, and the others were teenagers. Yeah, we just kept going.

"We lost two citizens in the city because of the flood. One man put his truck on higher ground. As he walked back to his house, the undercurrent took him and slammed him against a fence, and he drowned. His wife has Lupus. We rescued her and a daughter. There was four and a half feet of water in the house. You know, when her skin touched the dirty [Harvey] water, it instantaneously blistered.

"I weigh 160 pounds. I'm not a big guy. And my brother-in-law, he's about the same. I don't know how we did it. One lady weighed more than 300 pounds. We carried her out and *put her on the tractor and got her to a safe place. I was using the brush hog. You know, a brush hog goes up and down on an agriculture tractor. I dropped it all the way down, put her on it, and I had some ropes. I tied her to the tractor because the current was heavy.*

"Thank God I know how to swim because we had to swim to some places. It was deep, man. It was crazy. The amount of water that the city took in was catastrophic. The current was crazy. It was real strong. It turned our tractor, not over, but sideways. It twisted it. Not flipped it over but turned it when we were crossing a bridge. The current was strong. It was like when you're whitewater rafting. It was like that. The waves that were getting broken by the cars and stuff in the bayou! ...

"The only light we had was the light from the John Deere tractor. The light that every tractor comes with. And, I had a half a tank of diesel, so that lasted a long time. I never filled it up. I ruined that tractor though. That $36,000 tractor was ruined. But that's no big deal. I didn't expect nobody to fix it.

"I was already starting to drain the oil when I got a phone call from Doggett equipment in Houston. They know me. I got my equipment from them. They had heard about my tractor. They said, 'Willie we want to fix your tractor. The CEO of John Deere is gonna call you.' I'm thankful for them. They fixed it like new. People here are thankful that I helped. I don't think it was so much that I helped, it was just that I was the only one that could help."

I deliberately held Willie's story until the end of this chapter. He represents most of us who are reading this book. He's busy with his family, his business, and his public service. He's never received any special training in rescue work. He's an "ordinary" guy like most of us. And, like thousands of others in the Metropolitan Houston Area during Harvey and its aftermath, he was called to do something. He stepped up and answered the call.

Despite facing significant danger to himself, Willie and his brother-in-law saw people in trouble, and they ran, swam and walked, in many cases, to help. This is noble behavior. A notable Philosopher once said, "There is no greater love than to lay your life down for another." If that statement is true, and I think it is, then we saw enormous love in our community during hurricane Harvey. **Houston brought the "love your neighbor" principle to life for all to see! As a result, can you hear the crumbling silos!**

CHAPTER 11

CRUMBLING SILOS

The Look of Crumbling Silos – People Waiting to Volunteer

CRACK!! SWOOSH!! SPLASH!! ... Did you hear it? Did you see it? Did you feel it? Do you hear it, see it, feel it now? Houston's ethically intelligent response to hurricane Harvey's death and destruction began collapsing the many silos into which we've segregated ourselves. I hope you heard it, saw it, and felt it because many of us did and do. These silos have inflicted great harm on our society. But, it's ending! The nearby photo says it all.

Local Houston talk show host Michael Berry tweeted this iconic photo during hurricane Harvey. The photo shows people from the Houston area lining up to volunteer their time and talent helping those who were adversely affected by the hurricane. If you examine the people standing in this line, you'll note that it reflects the diversity of this community. And, I can assure you, that when these people registered to help, they didn't specify a desire to help only those who were members of their "tribe" or who resided in their respective "silo."

Houston has shown the way to a new beginning. This chapter is about and celebrates that new beginning. So, prepare your mind, heart and spirit. The wave is coming to you and your tribe.

Mending the Hurt

As I complete this book, I remember my promise to Lori at the GRB Rescue Center as she and thousands of others tried to make sense of their circumstances. I promised her she wouldn't be forgotten. The publication of this book is the first step in fulfilling that promise.

As I write this final chapter, it's now tax time, April 2018. It's been more than seven months since hurricane Harvey ravaged the Gulf Coast area. The national media moved on long ago. The local media has continued to provide periodic updates of our community's recovery, just enough to keep it more than a distant memory within local consciousness.

Despite the local media's best efforts, hurricane Harvey and its aftermath are slowly receding from even local memories. Yet, we still have thousands of displaced families living in temporary housing of one kind or another. We still have hundreds of volunteer groups rebuilding homes. Last Sunday, a friend at Lakewood Church, who is close to the Church's Harvey outreach initiative, told me that we still have hundreds of families living in unmucked damaged homes. This recovery is going to take years, not a few months.

As a gentle reminder of that reality, I've included two final stories of people and their families whose lives are still in limbo, not yet "recovered." All may not have recovered yet, but we know we will.

Here is Tony and Elsa's story of treadmill living after Harvey.

"We've lived in our home for a little over eight years. When we bought the home, we were told it was in the 500-year floodplain. So, we never felt the need to have flood insurance. Then, came the 2016 Tax Day flood. We had more than 3 feet of water in our home on that day. After that flood, we talked it over and decided it must have been a fluke of nature. So, we decided to use all of our savings, almost $85,000, and repair the home. We'd just completed the repairs and moved back in early in 2017.

"Then, came the Harvey flood, which was so much worse and absolutely devastating to our home. We had to

Home Gutted Again

be rescued by boat, and we lost everything. The water was so deep inside our house this time, it destroyed everything including personal keepsakes, clothing, and our entire kitchen. It happened so quickly, we were unable to save anything. So, here we are. The holidays are over. Life goes on, but it's like living in a hellish limbo.

"We moved into this small apartment with our two kids.

It's more than ten miles from our house. We chose this apartment because it's all we could afford. So, getting our kids to and from school and related activities, is a real hassle. Tony and I both have full-time jobs. He travels a lot in his job. So, most of the time, I am struggling to keep everyone going.

"Thankfully, insurance replaced both of our cars, and our employers really worked with us as we made these adjustments. I don't know what's going to happen. We had no flood insurance. A church group gutted our house for us. But now, it's just setting empty. We have no money to repair it, and were not sure the authorities will allow us, anyway.

"We applied for assistance, but our applications were rejected because we make "too much money". That's also the attitude we get from our mortgage company. They seem to think we should easily be able to continue making our mortgage payment while renting this apartment and spending a fortune on gas and tolls. That side of things was okay until after Christmas. Now, most people's attitude is, 'It's been seven months since the flood. Everything is back to normal.' In our case, there is nothing **normal** about where we are! Being rescued by boat was the least worse part of hurricane Harvey for us."

> "… there is nothing **normal** about where we are! Being rescued by boat was the least worse part of hurricane Harvey for us."

Elsa and Tony are standing at the counter in their tiny apartment's kitchen eating dinner from paper plates, using plastic utensils. Even though, between the two of them, they earn over six figures, they're barely making it. Except for new clothing and a few personal items for their children, they've been unable to replace anything they've lost. Even the furniture in their small apartment is rented. They feel like they're on a treadmill going nowhere, and they don't know how to get off.

Small businesses were hit particularly hard by hurricane Harvey. Thousands are still struggling to get back on their feet, and thousands more have simply gone out of business. Small businesses are particularly vulnerable to sudden natural catastrophes. They have few extra resources, limited access to capital and, typically, are reliant on a handful of major customers. This small oil services firm's story is typical.

> *"Business was just startin' to really pick up again. With the low oil price and all of the downsizing and layoffs in the energy business, our little service company struggled for the last couple of years. July [2017] was the best month we'd had since the downturn began. It was still less than a third of what we were doing during the good times. But, it was good enough to give us hope again. We could pay the bills, and we had enough left over to begin some marketing.*
>
> *"Then, Harvey hit. We didn't flood and none of our folk's homes flooded. But, most of our customers took a big hit from the water. Plants and offices were closed for weeks. Our business just stopped, like someone had flipped a switch. We tried to keep payin' people, but that couldn't last very long. We got a few jobs, but it was just enough to keep the lights on. Then, I got sick.*
>
> *"Jenny said it was the stress. Maybe it was. I was worried about keepin' the house. God knows when you own your own business, you're the last to get paid. I finally had to go into the hospital for some tests. They found a small problem that needed minor surgery. It went fine, and I came back home after only a few days. When I signed on to my email, I had a slew of messages from my bank.*

"It looked like a small auto draft came through the account while I was in the hospital. I tried to stop all that stuff, since we were running so close to zero in the bank. Audrey used to take care of these details, but I had to let her go after we couldn't pay her. It looked like the bank had charged us over $200.00 in fees for a $45.00 item. I've got to tell you, right now $200.00 is a lot of money to us.

"So, I called and asked my bank officer and related what had happened and asked for a refund of the fees. My bank officer told me—and I kid you not—that the three-month disaster period the bank had established after the hurricane had ended. So, I wasn't eligible for a refund. I was speechless! At first, I was very angry. Then, I just broke down and started crying. I couldn't believe what was happening. Jenny said it was probably the drugs they gave me in the hospital.

"No! I was really hurt. I'd been with that bank for over nine years. I'd borrowed money and paid off several loans, never late with a single payment. My account was never in the red, and I conducted my business with integrity. Then, nothing. Now that it looked like my business was down and maybe out. They had no use for me or my business.

"The good news is we're still here! Our business is slowly coming back. As of last week, the price of crude oil is back over $60.00. People are startin' to feel more confident. One of my customers just announced a tax cut bonus for all employees. One of their buyers told me not to worry. They'd *take care of us. So, yeah. The rest of 2018 for us looks good.*

"In response to your original question, I would tell everyone that there are still a lot of folks who were hurt by the storm who are not back to normal. In our case, by July I'm hopin' we'll be back to where we were last July before Harvey."

There's still much to do helping everyone in this community not only return to where they were before the storm but also with a new vision and hope for the future. Both of the two previous stories are not simply tales of physical loss. Both of those stories, and thousands more like them, have a nonmaterial dimension. Often, we tend to overlook the mental, psychological and spiritual aspect of our human nature. Roy Wooten, Executive Director of Shield Bearer, described this neglect.

"People will devote time to watching those who are rebuilding their homes. People will devote time to going shopping for things they need to replace in their homes. They'll go to classes and meetings to learn how they can prevent it from ever happening to their home again or access funding from insurance or FEMA of non-profits or whatever. But they really have a hard time investing in themselves enough to come spend a day just focused on themselves.

Roy and his organization have developed a program called Hope After Harvey Survivors Workshop especially designed to help Harvey survivors restore this aspect of their lives. For those who can't pay the nominal fee to attend the workshop, it's free.

Births are often a precursor to important change.

A Harbinger

Here is a story of new birth and hope amid the storm. Jason Ryan is Director, U.S. Media Affairs, BP America, and here's his story.

On that weekend, I kept watching the weather reports. There I was with five and four-year-old boys and a very pregnant wife. We live in West University. On that Saturday and Sunday [August 26th and 27th] the water was over the curb on our street. Our neighbors had their kayak out going down the street.

It was very stressful. I spent Monday night in my son's room so I could watch the water. I didn't really sleep. My wife had to go in for appointment on Tuesday. She has type 1 diabetes and her pregnancy was deemed high risk. She was scheduled for a checkup. I have a pickup truck, and I had pre-driven the route the day before, just to make sure I could get through the water to the hospital.

We went in for the checkup. The doctors did some monitoring and said—it's time! By 1 o'clock, we were in the operating room. Twenty minutes later, here came baby girl Ryan. It was very emotional.

I'm a former TV news journalist, and I was watching the news coverage. I saw people going through so much suffering and everything else that's covered on the news these days. We saw so many rescues and, then, that family that was swept away in their van, including four children. It was just devastating. Then, just to have this little helpless new life emerge was just overwhelming. It was very overwhelming. The first time that I held her, was in the NICU.

The nurses in the NICU were like, 'Sir are you OK?' I was thinking, yeah, 'I'm great.' I'm good. It was pretty remarkable!

Jason's journey to the birth of his new daughter during hurricane Harvey, is a harbinger of hope for our community and our nation. We have the opportunity of exchanging the death, destruction and debris hurricane Harvey left us for the beauty of a less divided and polarized community and country. **We are on the cusp of a goodness revolution beginning right here in Houston, Texas!**

> We have the opportunity of exchanging the death, destruction and lingering debris hurricane Harvey left us for the beauty of a less divided less polarized community and country.

Birthing a Goodness Revolution

In his 1962 book, *The Structure of Scientific Revolutions,* Thomas Kuhn wrote about how science is incremental, until it's not. The book is about paradigms. More specifically, Kuhn's book is about paradigms of understanding.

We create paradigms or, models if you will, to explain something or help us understand a phenomenon. Kuhn described several instances of scientific paradigms that were accepted as "settled" science. Then, someone made a discovery or a series of discoveries and completely shattered the previous paradigm. The prior paradigm of understanding simply crumbled given the new paradigm's better suitability for modeling reality.

> We are on the cusp of a goodness revolution beginning right here in Houston, Texas!

One of the most significant scientific examples was the discovery of the quanta and the birth of quantum theory. Up until that time, the principles of Newtonian physics governed our understanding of nature. Quantum theory had upended the old Newtonian paradigm and added greatly to our understanding of reality.

We have contemporary examples. Advertising and marketing is one. Since the advent and growth of social media, advertising paradigms have completely changed. Where once there was print and broadcast media, we now have a plethora of channels through which we can directly reach our targeted audience. As in these paradigms, our contemporary silo/tribal paradigm of carving our society into smaller and smaller slices must end.

How We Got Here. Let's take a short trip down my memory lane. As I have mentioned previously, I have lived a blessed long life. I have known, or at least been exposed to, seven generations of people— 1) Unnamed - my grandparents; 2) Greatest - my parents; 3) Silent - my wife and I; 4) Baby Boomers - my brothers; 5) Gen-X - my children; 6) Millennials - three of my grandchildren; 7) Gen-Z - two of my grandchildren.

I came of age in the 1950's. I grew up in the "Nifty" fifties. I have many fond memories of that time, the music – doo-wop, Elvis, Chuck Berry, the Supremes, the cars – especially the 1957 Chevy convertible, sock hops, the birth of fast food, TV shows like *I Love Lucy* and Dick Clark's *American Bandstand*. There was the dark side too. Separate but equal was never right, and its demise began when I was a teenager.

I began my undergraduate studies as an engineering student at the University of Detroit the year after John F. Kennedy was inaugurated president. His presidency ushered in a newly optimistic time in our country. In 1962, Detroit was a thriving and welcoming city. It was a fun place to live, and you could go anywhere using the DSR. Crime may have been a problem, but my colleagues and I never noticed.

I left Detroit in 1966 to pursue an MBA degree. I returned to the city in late 1967, just after the infamous riots. The city to which I returned was radically different. The riots had torn the fabric of the city asunder. Hate invaded the city during those two years and has never departed. Neighborhoods that were previously serene and peaceful became islands of suspicion and fear. Entire sections of the city resembled the bombed-out neighborhoods of Dresden after the World War II.

It was during the 1960s, that violence became an acceptable form of public discourse. We reverted to old-world methods of eliminating leaders we didn't like—Medgar Evers, 1963, John F. Kennedy, 1963, Malcom X, 1965, Martin Luther King, Jr. 1968, Robert F. Kennedy, 1968, all assassinated. Anti-Vietnam war protesters used violence as their tool of choice, occupying universities and businesses destroying property wherever they went.

The Democratic National Convention in Chicago in 1968 was beset with unprecedented violence. Then, the carnage reached a climax at Kent State University in May 1970, where members of the Ohio National Guard opened fire on a group of protesters, killing four and wounding nine. Our nation took a collective deep breath hoping this sobering event would bring an end not only to the violence but also the rips that were appearing in our country's social fabric.

These societal tears weren't simply the result of ethnic or racial tensions. The Vietnam War created two new groups of people, the drafted and the deferred. Those who were drafted and served were treated like dirt when returning from the war. Those with deferments were called draft dodgers who possessed little to no patriotism. Both groups silently disliked and distrusted each other.

The United States of America lost on all fronts of the Vietnam War. The societal wounds created by that war persist. Is this the moment our country reversed its long historical march to unity? Okay! I see the eyes rolling and hear the murmuring under the breath. You're thinking I'm just some old guy pining for the "good ole days." In some respects, you would be correct.

I think it was a good thing when fathers earned enough to support their family, and moms had a choice about going to work outside the home. It was a good thing when children could take long walks to and from school with no worries about their safety. It was also a good circumstance when children could play outside all day long with little supervision because neighbors looked out for neighbors.

I also think it was more desirable that when immigrants came to this country, they had an insatiable desire to become Americans. When they arrived, they left their old country behind and embraced their new country. We didn't have hyphenated Americans. My mother never called herself a Polish–American. My father never called himself a Romanian–American. They were Americans. I am told that my grandparents insisted their children learn to speak English.

Earlier immigrants to this country had no better time of it than those coming today. They were looked down upon. They were considered dirty and uncouth. They were given pejorative names like wop, spic and hunky. They were given the lowest of low jobs. My paternal grandfather worked 12-hour days six days a week next to a blast furnace in a steel mill for less than five dollars a week.

As far as I know, he had no formal education. But, just two generations later, most of his grandchildren have college degrees and prosperous families. The promise of a better life in America hasn't changed. If that is true, what has changed?

There are too many small factors to enumerate. And, that may be the subject for another book. But, I digress. **There's only one factor that matters—leadership**. We've come to tolerate failed leaders. We have leadership failures at all levels of society. Select any sector of our society that you might like, and I can show you failed leaders. Too many of our leaders have lost their way.

I know you're thinking, *how do failed leaders divide our society?* It's simple. **They don't lead everyone.** They lead their group, clique or tribe. And, to compensate for their failed leadership, they seek to divide and conquer. They pit one slice of Americans against another, which is one of the reasons the slices are getting smaller and smaller. Our leaders are becoming smaller and smaller.

> There's only one factor that matters—leadership. We've come to tolerate failed leaders. We have leadership failures at all levels of society.

Business as Usual is Over. The paradigm has shifted. The shift began right here in Houston Texas. During hurricane Harvey and its aftermath, we saw not only ethical intelligence displayed by countless thousands of ordinary people but also ethically intelligent leadership. That combination produced a unity of purpose and commitment hardly ever seen these days. The silos that contained our tribes crumbled to the ground, washed away as hurricane Harvey's floodwaters flowed away.

> The silos that contained our tribes crumbled to the ground, washed away as hurricane Harvey's floodwaters flowed away.

I end this chapter and book with this insightful statement from Houston Chief of Police, Art Acevedo.

> *"When the chips were down, the most diverse city in the nation, in the most diverse nation on earth, was a model of*

courage, a model of generosity and a model of unity. Some leaders, for political reasons, try to paint ethnic groups, religious groups, people based on national origin, socio-economic standing or the color of their skin ... they can try to paint folks with broad brushes. But, what I saw in this great melting pot we call Houston, Texas was the best of humanity.

"And that gives me great hope. Because this city represents a snapshot of what this country is going to look like in twenty years. You're not going to stop that. No matter what the politics are, no matter what people think, you're not going to stop that. We're a multicultural, multi-ethnic melting pot. It's what's made this country great. We saw the greatness of that rich diversity on display, and we should all be proud of that."

Exhausted Sheriff Deputy

There's an adage that says a picture is worth a thousand words. I present you such a picture of a Harris County Deputy Sheriff who had collapsed from exhaustion helping people. Sheriff Gonzalez told me that not long after this photo was taken, he saw this deputy back in the field helping people. This deputy's commitment to his community should remind us all of our obligations as members not only of this community but also humanity.

Let us all recommit ourselves to our unofficial national motto: *E. Pluribus Unum*

OUT OF MANY, ONE

CONCLUSIONS AND RECOMMENDATIONS

Researching and writing this book has gifted me with a unique perspective about hurricane Harvey, its aftermath and its profound impact on the greater Houston area. I've been privileged to interview survivors, first responders, civilian rescuers, volunteers, business leaders, media, and those public officials most directly responsible for our community's governmental response to the storm.

Although the nearly ten months of total immersion in all aspects of this event certainly don't qualify me as an "expert" in any of the many areas of professional emergency management, I am in a unique position to connect some dots whose connection are not obvious to anyone who hasn't had this experience. Whether it was weeping with a traumatized survivor whose fear and foreboding was palpable or talking to the sheriff or chief of police about the incredible heroism of their officers, I've absorbed an experiential mosaic accessible only to someone who has walked in these shoes.

Add the additional considerations that I am an experienced consultant and researcher, I feel duty-bound to offer a few conclusions and recommendations based on my unique "experiential mosaic." In doing so, I can assure that I don't have an agenda or cause informing what I say. I brought completely novice eyes, ears and fresh empathy to this project. With those caveats, here are my conclusions and recommendations.

Conclusions

- Transporting traumatized survivors long distances to cavernous rescue centers like convention facilities and athletic facilities is not in the best interests of survivors. This provides a dehumanizing personal experience that further traumatizes the survivor. Providing security at such facilities drains valuable human resources from other badly needed areas of the event.
- Social media provided invaluable lifelines for people in distress and those wanting to assist them. The importance of social media will most likely continue to grow in the coming years and future emergency events.
- Crowdsourced rescuing is going to grow in scope and can become an important element is future emergency events.

Recommendations

- Far in advance of any potential emergencies, strategically identify and equip decentralized temporary rescue drop off points that could be activated quickly. Combine these temporary drop off points with a network of preapproved volunteer civilian rescue homes where survivors and their families could go for a short period. In such a setting, survivors could recover in a friendly home environment.
- Leaders at all levels must learn how to effectively apply social media technology within their emergency plans. The plans must be coordinated across agencies and citizen groups.
- Leaders of governmental units must become comfortable with and welcome crowdsourced rescue assets, includ-

ing the people who own them. The cost of preparing for unknown future emergencies is far outside the bounds of taxpayer's willingness or ability to pay. Crowdsourcing may be the answer to quickly scalable emergency responses.

HARVEY HEROES AKA "THE UNSUNG"

♦

In the following paragraphs, you'll find selected vignettes of ordinary people and organizations who became extraordinary unsung heroes during hurricane Harvey. You may or may not have heard or read about them. So, I'm recognizing them here.

This list could contain thousands of names. Because of space constraints, I've necessarily limited it to a few. I personally selected the unsung heroes on this list. My criteria was simple—have they already been recognized in another public forum? If so, they probably aren't on this list. There are some exceptions. Here are the Harvey Heroes, presented in alphabetic order by last or organization name.

- **Arts Community of Houston** is an amazing, talented and selfless group of people and organizations who toil endlessly preserving and advancing Houston's art legacy. Houston's art community suffered a severe blow from hurricane Harvey's floods, nearly $90 million in losses by some accounts. I chronicle and celebrate the Houston Grand Opera's struggle to stay on course and present a complete 2017-18 season in this book. We should also recognize the many other arts companies who are standing strong and recovering. Our community is indebted to these dedicated but unsung heroes of this tragic event.

- **BakerRipley** is a Houston-based organization dedicated to doing good. When I asked him for his brightest moment during hurricane Harvey, Harris County Judge Ed Emmett said, "if I had to pick one thing I would say when we were asked to set up a shelter that could handle up to 10,000 people, and we contacted Baker-Ripley, which used to be known as Neighborhood Centers. That shelter [NRG Center] was set up in less than six hours and became the model shelter for the world and will probably be the model going forward. They know what they're doing, and they're very good at it. You know, that's a very positive thing to take out of this storm."

- **David Breslauer** is my friend, colleague and business partner, in that order. As you can imagine, in researching and writing this book, I accumulated hours and hours of audio. For me to use that audio, it had to be transcribed. As a researcher, I've had to transcribe interviews. I know how difficult and time consuming it is. Selflessly, Dr. Breslauer volunteered for that task and performed an incredibly boring, tiring and tedious task with excellence and only occasional complaining! This book wouldn't be what it is without his exemplary work.

- **Cajun Navy** is an informal volunteer force of people with small boats and other rescue equipment that helps people in need. The group's mission statement reads, in part, "We don't wait for the help, We are the help! We the people of Louisiana refuse to stand by and wait for help in the wake of disasters in our state and the country. We rise up to unite and help rescue our neighbors! Our mission is to help the people who can't get help, not only in the wake of disaster, but in everyday life. From the under privileged, the homeless, and all veterans in this country, we won't stand by and watch another person suffer, struggle, and fight for their lives, while the world passes by. We're here to do something about it and make a real change in the lives of many." The Cajun Navy may be made up of folks from Louisiana, but they came to help Houston during Harvey.

- **Trish Conley** and Helena Fyda are Human Resources Vice Presidents for BP America in Houston and Chicago respectively. They played critical behind-the-scenes roles in helping BP America's Houston employees as hurricane Harvey ravaged the Houston area. According to Cindy Yeilding of BP, both women were amazing resources during the storm helping others. Most of those helped by Helena's and Trish's efforts will never know their names—until now!

- **Stephanie Coulter** is a Houston cardiologist. In fact, she's my cardiologist, and an excellent one at that! She is Program Director of The Texas Heart Institute (THI) Cardiovascular Disease Fellowship at Baylor St. Luke's Medical Center. Dr. Coulter and her THI Fellows provided critical medical care during hurricane Harvey. Isolated at the Medical Center due to Harvey's flood waters, these doctors worked their life-saving skills despite their own families being in peril in flooded homes and neighborhoods. Yes! It's their job to save lives, but we should never forget the selfless sacrifices these doctors made. Their only complaint—the hospital food!

- **Sammy Dobbs, III**, risking his own personal truck and other resources, worked with a rescue boat crew first in the Houston area and then in the Beaumont, Port Arthur and Orange, Texas. Endangering his life and safety, Sammy worked 14-16-hour days with little rest helping people escape Harvey's aftermath. Even if he wasn't my son-in-law, I'd be proud of this man and his character.

- **Chris Garcia** is a former MBA student of mine. His mother lives not far from the Brazos River, and she had recently been widowed. Her house was overrun by the Brazos River, swollen from Harvey's rains. While it was still raining, Chris and several of his colleagues from work set about mucking out her house and getting it ready for rebuilding. Anyone who takes care of his mama like this, deserves to be called an unsung hero.

- **Bob Harvey** is President and CEO of the Greater Houston Partnership. His quiet, understated and behind-the-scenes leadership during hurricane Harvey cries out for recognition. Behind the scenes, Bob worked tirelessly as a go-between for those seeking resources and those possessing resources. Bob selflessly used his substantial "Rolodex" connecting those who needed help with those who could help. One shining example was a request from the Houston Independent School District for IT professionals to visit each school, make whatever repairs were necessary and bring the school back online. Bob sent out a request, and more than 300 IT professionals responded. In fact, Bob had so many volunteers, he had to turn many away. Thank you, Bob Harvey, for toiling in anonymity helping our community and for contributing to this book's success.

- **Houston Firefighters Who Became Momentary Seals** is a group of firefighters responding to a house fire during hurricane Harvey's flooding. The house was located on a street covered by four feet of floodwater. When the firefighters reached the burning house, the fire hydrant was under that four feet of water. The team had to dive under the water to connect their hose to the fire hydrant. Once the water was flowing through the hoses, the firefighting team made their way to the house and started pouring water onto the fire. This incident is one of the hundreds of ironies emerging from hurricane Harvey. Here we have a house on fire surrounded by water. I don't know the names of the firefighters on this team, but they're certainly all unsung heroes.

- **Houston's Religious Community** responded fast and mightily to the human suffering in our community because of hurricane Harvey's flooding. I've been told that 80% of the aid to Harvey survivors in the weeks immediately following the event came from Houston's religious community. There were so many different religious communities involved, I simply couldn't list them all. One survivor told me that the only people he saw in his neighborhood helping people were from area churches. So, we salute all who helped and are still helping as I write this in April 2018.

- **Michelle Hundley,** lives in Kingwood, and her home didn't flood. But, because of the flooding around her home, Michelle was unable to leave her home. So, using Zillow, she began dispatching the Cajun Navy to locations where people needed rescue. Even in her distressed circumstances, Michelle saw a community need and rose to the occasion filling that need. Harris County Judge Ed Emmett was so impressed with her work, he hired her!

- **Lakewood Church** is our church family. Linda and I have been members since 2003, and I'm going to brag on us a little. After receiving permission from the City of Houston, our church became a rescue center and, more importantly, a redistribution center for emergency supplies including clothing. We received and distributed multiple tons of supplies throughout the community. Our church fielded an army of 7,000 volunteers who helped clean over 1,000 houses in Harvey's aftermath. Our volunteers continue rebuilding houses and families and will continue such efforts until there is no longer a need. For this, Lakewood Church is an unsung hero!

- **John Mingé** is Chairman, Chief Executive Officer and President of BP America. Although not physically present in Houston during the initial flooding from hurricane Harvey, John empowered his Houston leadership team to effectively respond to the unfolding disaster. He also reached out to his Houston employees and approved a most generous package of benefits to those who suffered losses from hurricane Harvey. We don't often see this kind of "in the moment" courageous leadership from business leaders. For his caring and compassion about his community and employees, John Mingé is an unsung hero.

- **Andrew Pasek** made the ultimate sacrifice rescuing his sister's cat from a flooded home. He accidentally stepped on an electrified wire hidden under the flood water. Andrew was electrocuted, even while warning others to stay away and not try rescuing him.

- **Rebuilding Together Houston** is a local Houston charity that restores hope and revitalizes neighborhoods by repairing homes at no cost for low-income elderly homeowners, veterans and, now, hurricane Harvey survivors. Through the work of volunteers and with the support of public-and private-sector initiatives, they enhance the quality of life for deserving seniors, strengthen the communities in which they live, and build a brighter future for Houston. Rebuilding Together Houston is one of the designated organizations receiving the profits from this book.

- **Willie Rios** is mayor *pro tem* of the city of South Houston. During the worst of hurricane Harvey and its flooding, in pouring rain and howling winds, Willie and his brother-in-law rescued over 200 people using Willie's construction tractor. At one time, Willie and his helper had over 15 people clinging to the machine as they navigated water over five feet deep.

- **Melissa Rotholz** is Associate Director of Shield Bearer. When hurricane Harvey began flooding Houston, Melissa jumped into action helping neighbors. She and Director Wooten began visiting rescue shelters listening to people talk about their experiences. Simply engaging traumatized people in conversation may not seem like much, but, if they will talk, it helps relieve some of the internal stresses. Melissa and her organization continue helping hurricane Harvey survivors to this very day.

- **Shield Bearer** is a local Houston charity that is fighting for hearts of people, couples, families and adolescents as they battle to victory. Shield Bearer exists to help people struggling with personal, marital and family problems. Last year, Shield Bearer provided professional counseling services to over 7,000 hurting hearts without regard to ability to pay. Shortly after hurricane Harvey unleashed unrelenting rains and flooding, Shield Bearer stepped up and began helping people traumatized by the storm and its aftermath. The counselors at Shield Bearer began treating Harvey Brain before we had even named it! Shield Bearer [www.shieldbearer.org] is one of the designated organizations receiving the profits from this book.

- **TxDOT** the Texas Department of Transportation mobilized all 25 Districts and over 4,000 employees during hurricane Harvey and its aftermath. These dedicated public servants came from all over the state and worked 24/7, doing whatever was necessary in the rescue, recover and cleanup after the storm. This vital organization is truly one of the unsung heroes of hurricane Harvey.

- **Rod Windham** is Director of Political Sales for iHeartMedia Houston. During iHeart's nonstop hurricane Harvey storm coverage and because there was no trash service, Rod went around the facility and picked up the garbage every day. He hauled it out to his car. And, navigating flooded streets, Rod found dumpsters where he could leave the trash. Then he would stop at restaurants and pick up food for the staff. One of Rod's colleagues said, "He is one of the dearest people on our staff. A Vietnam War veteran, he's a leader in everything he does, and he became such an integral and necessary part of our existence for those eleven days."

- **Roy Wooten** is Executive Director of Shield Bearer. Roy said, "We didn't have anyone come ask us to get involved. As the storm continued in day two and day three, we started knowing that we needed to do what we've done before. We asked counselors if they were near shelters to go and do crisis counseling there. There's not a lot you can do in a crisis counseling situation except for helping them get through the day. To feel someone really gets my pain in some way is a very powerful gift and a healing thing." Roy and his organization continue helping hurricane Harvey survivors to this very day.

- **Cindy Yeilding** is Senior Vice President of BP America. John Maxwell, world renowned leadership expert, says leadership is, "Influence, nothing more, nothing less." Cindy epitomizes that definition. She organizes, collaborates, consults and then acts. She is quick to give credit to everyone on her team for its accomplishments. BP America's ethically intelligent response to hurricane Harvey's ravages in Houston, is due to her leadership. She wields her influence softly, and gets things done. She was committed to doing right for BP America and its extended family of employees and contractors in Houston. She succeeded. Her leadership style reminded me, again, of a famous quote, "It's amazing how much you can accomplish when you don't care who gets the credit." Thank you, Cindy, for setting an example for leaders everywhere. And because of that example, she is an unsung hero.

THE JOURNEY FROM TRUTH TO WISDOM GRAPHIC

This graphic is taken from my book, *Ethical Intelligence: The Foundation of Leadership.* It is a graphical representation of the steps, or levels, of attainment achieved on your journey to becoming an ethically intelligent person.

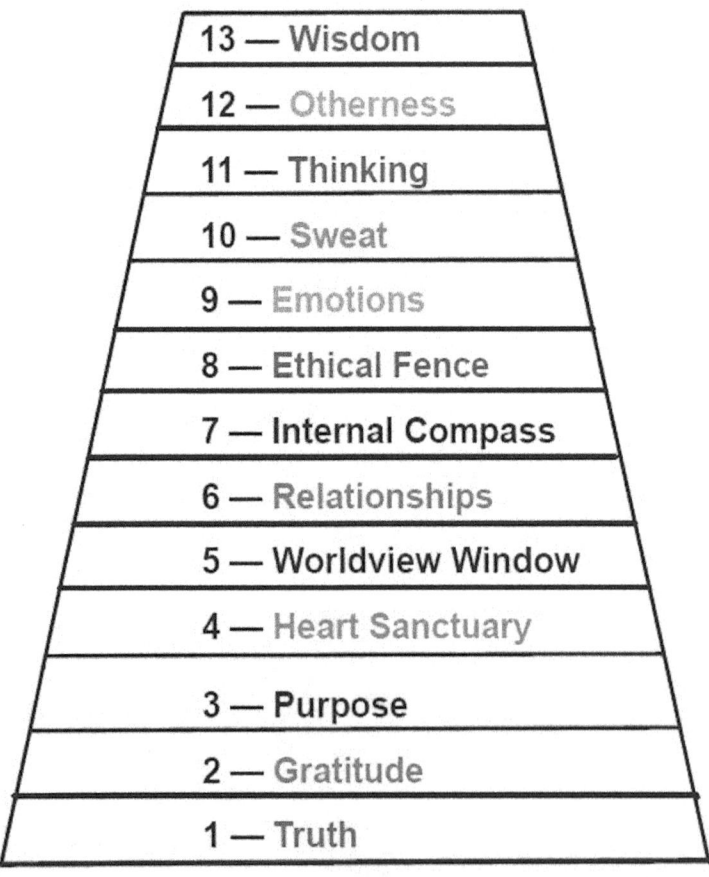

DISCUSSION QUESTIONS FOR US

Houston's response to hurricane Harvey and its aftermath presented many valuable lessons. One of my objectives in writing this book was to highlight those lessons with the hope that we might all learn some important truths about ourselves.

As you begin reading this book, ask yourself the following questions. Note your answers. Then, after you've read the book, return and ask yourself these same questions again.

- **How well do you see others? Do you see them clearly?**
- **Do you judge people before you know anything about them?**
- **Does the good of the many always outweigh the good of the few or, even, one?**
- **Is right or wrong negotiable during a crisis? Why or why not?**
- **Are there worthless people among us? Who or what determines worth? Do you care? Why or why not?**
- **Do you know your life's purpose? Are you pursuing it?**
- **Do your green field relationships outnumber your brown field relationships?**
- **Should those who prepare for emergencies receive more assistance recovering after the emergency than those who made no preparations? Is there a responsibility to prepare?**

- Benjamin Franklin once said, "We must all hang together or, assuredly, we shall all hang separately." Forgetting, for a moment, Franklin's context, what does this mean to you?
- Are we ever better off when our leaders lie to us? If you believe we are, under what circumstances is lying acceptable?
- Will you have the courage to walk away when your time comes?
- Do emotions rule your life? Why not?

PHOTO CREDITS

Pg	Description	Source
5	Houston Metropolitan Area Under Water	WikiMedia Commons
7	Downtown Houston at Dusk 2017	WikiMedia Commons
9	Houston Ship Channel	WikiMedia Commons
10	Texas Medical Center	WikiMedia Commons
11	Hurricane Harvey as Viewed from Space	U.S. Department of Defense
12	Hurricane Harvey Flood Water in Houston	WikiMedia Commons
15	Harvey Brains aka "The Moment"	Shutterstock - Stock
1	Rescuers Evacuating People from Flooded Homes	U.S. Department of Defense
2	Rooftop Flooding Near Author's Home	U.S. Department of Defense
3	Untitled	U.S. Department of Defense
19	View from Author's Garage	Author
21	Ducks in Author's Cul-de-Sac	Author
22	Author's Front Yard	Author
23	Author and His Dog Rocky	Author
24	Air Boats in Author's Neighborhood	Author
25	Helicopter Rescue from Author's Neighborhood	Author
27	Flooded Home In Author's Neighborhood	Author
29	George R. Brown Convention Center	WikiMedia Commons
30	George R. Brown Convention Center	New Hampshire Public Radio - Marisa Penaloza
31	George R. Brown Convention Center	Texas State Representative Gene Wu
33	Distraught Rescuee	U.S. Department of Defense
35	Flooded Greenspoint Townhouses	U.S. Department of Defense
40	Volunteers Serving Food to First Responders	U.S. Department of Defense

Pg	Description	Source
45	Rescuers Using a Small Boat	U.S. Department of Defense
47	Dump Truck Rescuing Survivors	Getty Images - Joe Raedle
53	Homeless Man	Shutterstock - Stock
56	Puppy Rescue	U.S. Department of Defense
58	Segregated Drinking Fountains	Flickr - Stock
63	Rescuers In a Boat	U.S. Department of Defense
65	Helicopter Medical Rescue	U.S. Department of Defense
67	National Guard Truck Rescue	Author
68	Rubber Boat Rescue	U.S. Department of Defense
71	National Guard Truck Rescue	Author
73	Flooded Parking Lot	U.S. Department of Defense
75	Rubber Boat Rescue	U.S. Department of Defense
78	Emergency Leadership Team	WikiMedia Commons
79	Samaritan's Purse Volunteers	Samaritan's Purse
80	Debris Lined Street	Shutterstock - Stock
82	Gratitude Hug	U.S. Department of Defense
84	Cathy Pam's Rescue	Dallas Morning News - Louis DeLuca
86	Beijing Smog	Shutterstock - Stock
87	Survivors In Line For Benefits	Click2Houston.com
89	Houston Police Chief Acevedo	Houston Police Department
91	Water Rescue	U.S. Department of Defense
92	Water Rescue with Dog in Boat	U.S. Department of Defense
93	Deputy Rescuing Two Children	Harris County Sheriff's Office
94	Civilian Rescue Boat	U.S. Department of Defense
99	Steve Perez Funeral	Houston Public Media
101	Sheriff Ed. Gonzalez	Harris County Sheriff's Office
105	Houston Mayor Sylvester Turner	WikiMedia Commons

PHOTO CREDITS.

Pg	Description	Source
106	Greenspoint Rescue	Lisandro Sanchez
113	Nikki Courtney and Scott Crowder	Nikki Courtney
114	Nikki Courtney Sleeping on Couch	Nikki Courtney
123	Grandmother and Grandson	Shutterstock - Stock
130	Stalled Car	U.S. Department of Defense
142	We Can Get Through This, Too	FEMA
143	Mucked Out House	WikiMedia Commons
152	Flooded Stairwell	Houston Grand Opera
163	Leadership News Conference	KHOU-TV Houston
174	Hurricane Harvey Track	U.S. Department of Defense
176	Flood Waters	U.S. Department of Defense
178	Walking In Flood Water	U.S. Department of Defense
181	Widespread Flooding in Houston	WikiMedia Commons
183	Unprecedented Rooftop Flooding	WikiMedia Commons
186	Sandbagged House	Dr. Cesare Wright
188	Dog In Live Vest	Dr. Cesare Wright
191	Man Underwater	Shutterstock - Stock
193	Instant Flooding in Neighborhood	Dr. Cesare Wright
195	Flood Control Map	Harris County Flood Control District
196	Quickly Flooded Home	U.S. Department of Defense
199	Barker Dam Release	Houston Public Media - Gail Delaughter
209	La Traviata Promotion	Houston Grand Opera, Lynn Lane
215	Flood Damage at HGO	Houston Grand Opera
216	Flooded Kitchen	Dr. Cesare Wright
223	Flooded BP America Facility	BP America
224	Flooded BP America Facility	BP America

Pg	Description	Source
225	Flooded BP America Facility	BP America
233	The Look of Crumbling Silos	www.itsnothouitsme.com
235	Mucked Out House	U.S. Department of Defense
246	Collapsed Deputy Sheriff	Harris County Sheriff's Office

ABOUT THE AUTHOR

Dr. John Opincar, CPA, CGMA, serves as President and CEO of Boardroom Partners, a board-level consultancy. He is Associate Professor in the MBA program at the Jack Welch Management Institute and President and CEO of the Ethical Intelligence Research Center, a nonprofit research and educational institute. His current professional pursuits are all directed toward making the world a better place through research, writing, speaking and teaching about human ethical intelligence—one person and one organization at a time.

Previously, Dr. Opincar served as Campus and Academic Director for the University of Phoenix in Iowa. Since joining the University of Phoenix in 2003, he also served as Director of Academic Affairs in Iowa, Lead Faculty/Area Chair in Houston, and Associate Faculty member in Iowa, Houston, and Online Campuses. Dr. Opincar continues his role as a University of Phoenix associate faculty member. He previously held teaching posts at Belhaven University and Our Lady of the Lake University.

Prior to entering higher education, Dr. Opincar built a successful multi-decade career in business with large enterprises such as Deloitte Touche, PriceWaterhouseCoopers, and Ford Motor Company. He also founded and led several startups, the last of which was housed in the Technology Incubator at the University of Texas at Austin.

During his career, Dr. Opincar served in numerous business and higher educational leadership positions, including Chief Academic Officer at the University of Phoenix, CFO of a NYSE energy company, managing director of an international software consortium, board member and advisor, senior consultant to a select group of Fortune 500 clients and their directors and CEO of several privately held companies.

Dr. Opincar earned degrees from the University of Detroit Mercy, Michigan State University and the University of Phoenix. He is a lifetime member of Alpha Sigma Nu, Beta Alpha Psi, Beta Gamma Sigma and Delta Mu Delta honor societies. Dr. Opincar is a Certified Public Accountant in Michigan and a Chartered Global Management Accountant. He is a certified John Maxwell Team leadership coach, trainer and speaker. His non-professional pursuits include gourmet cooking, music, politics, gardening and Standard Poodles.

Author's Contact Information
www.johnopincar.com
E-mail: john.opincar@boardroompartners.com
Phone: 346-444-2626

OTHER BOOKS BY THE AUTHOR

These books are available on Amazon, other online bookstores, and the author's website: www.johnopincar.com.

Author: Opincar, John T.
Year: 2016
Title: Ethical Intelligence: The Foundation of Leadership
Place Published: Houston, Texas
Publisher: Cultural Fire Press, LLC
ISBN: 978-0-9980890-0-3

Author: Opincar, John T.
Year: 2017
Title: Organizational Culture: A Force Fierce as Fire
Place Published: Houston, Texas
Publisher: Cultural Fire Press, LLC
ISBN: 978-0-9980890-8-9

Author: Opincar, John T.
Year: Forthcoming, summer 2018
Title: C-Suite Leadership: Voices From the Fire
Place Published: Houston, Texas
Publisher: Cultural Fire Press, LLC

Author: Opincar, John T.
Year: Forthcoming, winter 2019
Title: Ethical Intelligence: The Gift Living in Your Consciousness
Place Published: Houston, Texas
Publisher: Cultural Fire Press, LLC

CELEBRATING THE COMPASSION, CARING, AND

www.ingramcontent.com/pod-product-compliance
Lightning Source LLC
Chambersburg PA
CBHW070913030426
42336CB00014BA/2401